HERIT

A TASTE OF BRITAIN

CW00481548

99p

ISBN 1 900327 59 7 paperback

A CIP catalogue record for this book is available from the British Library.

Cartographer: David Fryer
Designer: Ian Drury
Contributor: Alan Lovelock

Printed and bound in Spain.

Published by
West One (Trade) Publishing Ltd
Kestrel House
Dukes Place
Marlow
Buckinghamshire
SL7 2QH.

Telephone: 01628 487722
Fax: 01628 487724
E-mail: sales@west-one.com

Heritage Hotels – A Taste of Britain

Contents

Heritage Hotels – A Taste of Britain

Foreword

Given the diversity of history, cultures, landscapes and attractions in Great Britain, on the following pages we have attempted to epitomise "The Taste of Britain" by highlighting some of the more popular places that you can visit, and the things you can see and do. This is not designed to be a definitive tourist guide, but we hope it will help you to plan your holiday, a weekend break or a journey around our captivating isles.

Guy Crawford   Michel Bouquier

Our heritage is something of which we are rightly proud. Cathedrals, castles, manors and monuments bear witness to our architectural heritage, while our literary heritage hails from all over the country. But for a true "taste" of Britain, it is essential to sample our culinary heritage. Fresh Scottish salmon, delicious crumbly cheeses, Somerset cider and Kent strawberries will all make your stay truly memorable.

While you enjoy the tranquility and simplicity of picturesque villages, quaint fishing harbours and scenic landscapes, you should acquaint yourself with local specialities like Cornish pasties, Kendal mint cake, Cumberland sausages and the quintessentially British cream tea.

We hope you will have an enjoyable time with us, in whichever hotel you choose, and wherever you wander.

Cordially yours,

Guy Crawford
Managing Director
Heritage Hotels

Michel Bouquier
Marketing Director
Heritage Hotels

THE VERY ESSENCE OF BURGUNDY

"THE WINES OF THIS GREAT BURGUNDY HOUSE CONSISTENTLY PROVE THEIR UNMISTAKABLE CLASS."

TOM STEVENSON

Taste of Britain - a festival of food and drink

A Taste of Britain's country fare

**For more information contact: (0)870 400 8855
or visit www.heritage-hotels.com**

Heritage Hotels extends you a warm welcome at all of our restaurants.

Throughout 2000, Heritage is paying homage to our culinary heritage with a festival of month-long food events. Using only the freshest quality produce sourced from all over the country each month our chefs will be presenting a favourite British dish. Our menu features such delights as tender British lamb and mint sauce, classic rib eye steak and the summer taste of strawberries and champagne.

In addition to the pleasures of dining in one of our restaurants, we have included on the following pages some suggestions as to where you may seek out some of the best in local produce, wines, spirits and beers. Listing all the many hundreds of farm shops and food retailers is beyond the scope of this guide, but we hope that these ideas will give you a flavour of the events and markets available.

While every effort has been made to provide accurate information regarding attractions and events, timings and dates are liable to change, and certain producers make a charge to customers for visits.

Taste of Britain

March
The Big Red
A 12-oz. prime British rib-eye steak on the bone, served with chips and Bearnaise sauce, £9.95

April
The Honourable British Pudding
A choice of main courses followed by a delicious helping of traditional pudding, £7.95

May
The Great British Cheese Feast
Half a pound of assorted British cheeses, served with warm, crusty bread, apple, celery and chutney, £6.50

June
Celebrating British Lamb
A succulent rack of British lamb, served with minted new potatoes, £9.95

July
Just strawberries and champagne
Select from our strawberry fantasy menu (minimum half a pound of strawberries) and a glass of champagne, £8.50

August
From River and Sea
A magnificent salmon and crab salad with a glass of chilled Chardonnay, £8.95

Treasures of the West Country

A fine food and drink heritage trail through the South-West counties of Somerset, Devon and Cornwall

Stay at any of these Heritage Hotels:

The Bath Spa
Bath, see page 54

The Francis
Bath, see page 56

The Southgate
Exeter, see page 82

The Luttrell Arms
Dunster, see page 78

The Metropole
Padstow, see page 118

The Dart Marina
Dartmouth, see page 72

Few corners of our green and pleasant land offer such a wealth of fine produce as these three counties. No resource is left untouched - climate, sea, coast, river, meadow, moorland - all are exploited with traditional skills and anything but compromise.

World famous cheeses from Cheddar, fine herds of Jersey cows, many locally crafted ales, cider and West Country wine, and of course the famous Cornish pasty and clotted cream all add up to legendary culinary delights.

Avalon Vineyard, *The Little House, East Pennard:* Organic vineyard and fruit farm; self-guided vineyard walk; free wine & cider tasting, 01749 860393

Bridge Farm, *East Chinnock, Yeovil:* Cider, jams, pickles and fruit cakes made with apples or cider; conducted tours by appointment, 01935 862387

The Smokery, *Bowdens farm, Hambridge, Langport:* Traditional smokery in an old cider barn, producing a wide range of smoked foods; see the smoking process, and even bring your own salmon or trout for smoking, 01458 250875

Cheddar Gorge Cheese Company, *The Cliffs, Cheddar:* The only cheese producer to make cheddar cheese where it all began; see the cheese making process, and a cheesemaker is available to answer questions, *(Mar-Oct)* 01934 742810

Dunster Watermill, *Mill Lane, Dunster:* A fully restored 17th century working watermill producing stone-ground wholemeal flour and home-made muesli, *(Mar-Oct),* 01643 821759

Frances Kitchen Cooking Courses, *Stoney Mead, Curry Rivel, Langport:* One-day demonstration courses in a country house kitchen, 01458 251203

Harveys Cellars, *12 Denmark Street, Bristol:* Museum and diplays housed in the medieval cellars of the famous wine merchants; individual tours including a free glass of Harvey's Bristol Cream *(adults)*; guided tours; tutoring on port, sherry or table wine, and tastings for groups, 0117 927 5036

Trout farm, *Muddiford:* Catch your own trout, 01271 344533

Quince Honey Farm, *North Road, South Molton:* Visit one of the world's largest collections of living honeybees *(Easter-Oct);* at production times the whole process of honey extracting, filtering and bottling can be viewed, 01769 572401

Roskilly's Ice Cream, *Tregellast Barton Farm, St Keverne, Helston:* see the milking of the farm's Jersey herd, and then watch ice cream, clotted cream, fudge and truffles produced; guided tours, 01326 280479

The Lizard Pasty Shop, *Beacon Terrace, The Lizard, Helston:* Ann Muller's famous pasties made on the premises, and the art of pasty making can be frequently watched in the shop, 01326 290889

Local events:

March:
West Country Game Fair,
Royal Bath & West Showground,
Shepton Mallet, Somerset,
01749 822 200
April:
Taste of the West
Food & Drink Show,
Westpoint, Exeter,
01392 4407458,
Boscastle Beer Festival,
Boscastle, Cornwall,
01840 250 202
May:
West Cornwall Festival of Food,
Penzance, 01736 3623416,
Devon County Show,
Westpoint, Exeter,
01392 44477726
June:
Royal Bath & West of England
Show, Shepton Mallet,
Somerset 01749 822200,
Royal Cornwall Show,
Wadebridge, 01208 812183
July:
Mevagissey Feast Week,
Mevagissey, Cornwall, 01726
74014
August:
St Keverne Ox Roast,
St Keverne, Cornwall,
01326 28048727,
Newlyn Fish Festival,
Newlyn, Cornwall, 01736 363499
September:
Tamarisk 2000 Festival of
Cornish/Celtic heritage and
culture, Newquay,
Cornwall, 01637 854020
October:
Callington Honey Fair,
Callington, Cornwall,
01579 350230
Apple or Pumpkin Day at RHS
Rosemoor Garden, Torrington,
Devon, 01805 62406722

Cumbria

*A fine food and drink heritage trail through
the Lake District and Cumbria*

**Stay at any of these
Heritage Hotels:**

The Swan
Grasmere, see page 86

The Old England
Windermere, see page 142

Leeming House
Ullswater, see page 138

Cumbria's heritage is enshrined in the history of rugged
Cumberland and Westmorland - hams, lambs and one of the
world's most distinctive sausages.

Affordable comfort foods dominate the traditional Cumbrian
table, including many sweet offerings, like Cumberland Rum
Nicky, Grasmere Gingerbread and Damson & Apple Tansy, made
with the celebrated damsons of Windermere.

Annette Gibbons Cookery,
Ostle House, Mawbray,
Maryport:
One-day cookery courses for small
groups, focussing on vegetarian food
and entertaining, 01900 881356

Bread-making at The Village
Bakery, *Melmerby, Penrith:*
Andrew Whitely's bread-making
course is run in his bakery,
01768 881515

Hawkshead Trout Farm,
The Boathouse, Hawkshead:
Trout fishery on the largest stocked
lake in the north-west of England,
015394 36541

Jennings Brewery, *The Castle*
Brewery, Cockermouth:
Long established traditional brewery
tour and sampling, 01900 827462

Kennedy's Fine Chocolates,
The Old School, Orton, Penrith:
Watch the production of
handmade chocolates at this small
family firm, 015396 24781

Muncaster Water Mill,
Ravenglass:
Watch a working water-powered
corn mill producing a range of
stone-ground organic flours and
oatmeals, 01229 717232

Thornby Moor Dairy,
Crofton Hall, Thursby, Cumbria:
Dairy producing both goats'
and cows' milk soft and hard
cheeses, daily except Sundays,
016973 45555

Water Mill at
Little Salkeld, *Penrith:*
Traditional 18th century corn mill
powered by water, producing a
wide range of organic flours and
other oat and cereal products, and
with regular cookery classes

Little Salkeld, *Penrith:*
Bread-making courses throughout
the year, plus advanced courses for
those interested in sourdoughs and
yeasted breads;
Nov courses on soups, jams and
chutneys, 01768 881523

Regular Markets,
Carlisle: general covered market,
Mon-Sat
Cockermouth Indoor Market:
Mon-Sat
Ulverston: general market,
Thu & Sat
Ulverston Farmers' Market:
Town Centre; 3rd Sat in month,
01695 554900

Local events:

April:
Damson Day, *Apr 15*
A celebration of Westmorland
damsons at damson blossom
time in the Lyth Valley. Produce
for sale, exhibitions, cookery
demonstrations at Memorial Hall,
Crosthwaite, 015395 68987
May:
Whitehaven Rum Festival,
May 29 Major one-day festival,
Whitehaven, 01900 829990
June:
Keswick Beer Festival,
Jun 2-3 More than 100 beers,
Keswick Rugby Club, Davidson
Park, Keswick, 017687 7541410
National Trust Cumbrian
Kitchen Fayre, Sample local
produce, traditional 18th century
food stalls in walled garden,
Wordsworth House, Main Street,
Cockermouth, 01900 824805
July:
Cumberland County Show,
Jul 15 Rickerby Park,
Carlisle, 01228 56036429
August:
Cartmel Agricultural Show,
Aug 2 Cartmel Park,
01539 72277710
September:
Ulverston Beer Festival,
Sep 2 Annual CAMRA event,
Coronation Hall, County Square,
Ulverston, 015394 33912
Westmorland County Show,
Sep 14 Lane Farm, Milnthorpe,
Crooklands, 015395 67804

Cotswolds Country

*A fine food and drink heritage trail through the
Cotswolds and Gloucestershire*

**Stay at any of these
Heritage Hotels:**

The Bear
Woodstock, see page 146

The Randolph
Oxford, see page 116

The Eastgate
Oxford, see page 114

The Queen's
Cheltenham, see page 66

After long walks through some of Britain's loveliest countryside,
it is extremely satisfying to settle down to simple, excellent food.
Delicious cheeses, chutneys and fruit, washed down with some
truly fine ale, make a perfect end to a tiring day.

Bibury Trout Farm,
Gloucester: Trout farm which breeds rainbow trout. See the developing trout in 20 ponds and feed the fish, 01285 740215

Cotswold Fudge,
1 Brewery Court, Cirencester: Watch fudge being traditionally hand-made from natural ingredients, 01285 653995

Smarts Traditional Gloucester Cheeses, *Old Ley Court, Chapel Lane, Birdwood Churcham:* The making of Double and Single Gloucester cheeses can be seen every Tuesday and Thursday *(Mar-Oct)*; call to arrange a visit on 01452 750225

Three Choirs Vineyard:
70 acre vineyard and winery; Newent Vineyard trail; wine tasting, exhibition and video show, 01531 890223

Ceci Paolo Cooking Classes, *High Street, Ledbury* - Courses for the enthusiast, 01531 632976

Cider Museum & King Offa Distillery, *Pomona Place, Whitecross Road, Hereford:* Original champagne cider cellars; cider brandy distillery; traditional cider making through the ages; sample the products from the distillery, 01432 354207

Dairy House, *Whitehill Park, Weobly, Herefordshire:* Small dairy making yoghurts, double and clotted creams, créme fraiche and fromage frais; visitors in groups by appointment, 01544 318815

Frome Valley Vineyard,
Bartestree, Hereford: Family run vineyard and garden in a lovely rural setting. Tour the vineyard and taste the wine; special arrangements made for parties (pre-book on 01432 850003)

H P Bulmer, *The Cider Mills, Plough Lane, Hereford:* Premier UK cider maker. A highlight of any tour is the cider mill (in season) where over 1000 tonnes of apples are processed daily; sampling; visits by appointment, 01432 352000

Astley Vineyards, *Astley, Stourport-on-Severn:* Producer of award winning estate grown white wines; Vineyard trail and wine tasting, 01299 822907

Barnfield Cider & Wine Mill, *Tuck Mill, Broadway:* Paris wine press (1920); two screw type wooden presses; six ton 1780 horse driven stone cider mill. Free tasting of cider, wines and other drinks, 01386 853145

Malvern Water Springs and Wells: Pouring forth natural mineral water. Various locations around Malvern. Help yourself!

Tina Boughey's Cookery School, *Sinton Green:* Demonstrations and cookery courses, 01905 640126

Local events:

May:
Cheese rolling at Randwick, Ancient custom; one of the cheeses is cut and shared after rolling; Randwick, Gloucester 01453 76678220
Bretforton Asparagus Auction & Concert, Brass band concert and asparagus auction, Bretforton, Worcester 01386 831872
June:
Agricultural Show, *Jun 17,* Three Counties Showground, Malvern, 01684 584900
July:
Beer Festival, *Jul 28-30* Postlip, Gloucester, 01242 522878
August:
Herefordshire Country Fair, *Aug 6* Deer Park, Eastnor Castle, Herefordshire, 01981 240168
Pershore Plum Fayre, Street fair displaying and selling arts and crafts, plums and plum-based foods, Pershore, 01386553605
September:
Ludlow Marches Food & Drink Festival, *Sep 8-10* Ludlow, 01746 7121059
Newent Onion Fair, Newent, Gloucester, 01531 8224689
Lindridge Beer Festival, Tenbury Wells, Ludlow, 01584 881689
The Malvern Autumn Show, *Sep 23-24* Three Counties Showground, Malvern, Worcester, 01684 58490028
October:
Cheesefest, Annual cheese festival and awards, Stow-on-the-Wold, 01594 812388
Ledbury Hop Fair, *Oct 9-10* Ledbury, Herefordshire, 01531 636147
Big Apple Weekend, *Oct 14-15* Much Marcle, Ledbury, Herefordshire, 01531 670544

15

Yorkshire

A fine food and drink heritage trail

Stay at The Black Swan, *Helmsley, see page 88*

Bass Brewery, *Tadcaster:*
The home of Stone's Best Bitter; evening tours Mon-Thu by appointment, 01937 832361

Big Sheep & Little Cow Farm, Aiskew: Small scale dairy farm See the farm at work and taste the ice-cream, 01677 422125

Black Sheep Brewery, Masham: Producer of award winning ales; visitors' centre with conducted tours, 01765 680100

Crakehall Water Mill, *Little Crakehall:* Fully restored water mill producing stone-ground flour. *(Easter-Sep)* 01677 422037

Cropton Brewery, *New Inn, Cropton:* Micro brewery producing award winning ales; visitors' centre, 01751 417330

Cuisine Eclairee, *Helmsley & other locations:* School run by professional, E Lemm. Speciality classes covering vegetarian and seasonal recipes, 01347 848557

Fountains Dairy Cheese Shop, *Lightwater Village, North Stainley:* Yorkshire's largest cheese shop; weekend cheese-making demonstrations, 01765 635445

Hazlewood Castle Cookery Classes, *Hazlewood:* Demonstrations on a variety of subjects with an emphasis on seasonal dishes, 01937 535353

John Smith Brewery, *Tadcaster:* Tour of brewery with tasting, 01937 832091

Leventhorpe Vineyard, *Woodlesford, Leeds:* One of the most northerly commercial vineyards in Europe, producing possibly the world's most northerly red; conducted tours by appointment, 0113 2667892

Moorland Trout Farms, *Newbridge, Pickering:* Walk around the trout farm and feed the fish, 01751 473101

Samuel Smith, *The Old Brewery, Tadcaster:* Yorkshire's oldest brewery. See the brewing process and visit the shire horse stables; by appointment only, 01937 832225

Wensleydale Dairy Products, *Hawes:* A creamery in the heart of the Dales, daily tours of the creamery, video, viewing gallery and cheese tasting, 01969 667664

Yorkshire Lavender, *Terrington:* Europe's most northerly lavender farm. *(Apr-Sep)* 01653 648430

Regular Markets, *Malton Farmers' Market:* Market Place, Malton; Tue 9am-2pm, 01751 473780

Skipton General Market: Mon, Wed, Fri, Sat 9am-5pm, 01756 792809

Helmsley General Market: Fri

Richmond General Outdoor Market: Sat 7.30am-4pm; indoor market Tue, Thu, Sat.

Local events:

January:
Wakefield Rhubarb Trail & Festival of Rhubarb, *Jan 13-15*
An unusual festival which includes a tour of the rhubarb forcing sheds at Carlton, special meals and a farmers' market at various venues, 01924 30584122-23
Traditional bread baking,
Colne Valley Museum, Cliffe Ash, Huddersfield; 01484 659762
February:
Rotherham Real Ale & Music Festival, *Feb 23-26* Rotherham, Over 100 real ales, 01709 512222
March:
Leeds Beer Cider & Perry Festival, *Mar 16-18* Civic Hall, Pudsey, 0113 255 8747
April:
World Dock Pudding Championship, *Apr 9* Elphaborough, Hebden Bridge 01422 883023
Doncaster Beerex 2000, *Apr 13-16* Doncaster, Over 80 real ales plus cider, 01302 563680
June:
Wetherby Agricultural Show, *Jun 4* Grange Park, 01937 833299
North Yorkshire County Show, *Jun 24* Otterington Hall, 01609 77020629
July:
Great Yorkshire Show, *Jul 11-13* Great Yorkshire Showground, Harrogate, 01423 54100025
August:
Wensleydale Agricultural Show, Leyburn, 01969 640261
September:
York Festival of Food & Drink, Major festival at various venues in York, 01904 554425
October:
Apple Week at Beningbrough Hall & Gardens, York, 01904 47066622

South East Counties

A fine food and drink heritage trail through the South-East counties of Surrey, Sussex and Kent

Stay at **The Kingston Lodge**, *Kingston, see page 96;* **The Burford Bridge**, *Box Hill, see page 58;* **The White Horse**, *Dorking, see page 74;* **The Chaucer**, *Canterbury, see page 64; or* **The Star Inn**, *Alfriston, see page 46*

Ringden Farm Apple Juice,
Hurst Green, East Sussex:
Farm pressed apple blends and single variety juices; visitors can sample the juice and see the product being made, 01580 879385

Seven Sisters Sheep Centre,
Eastbourne, East Sussex:
Dairy products made from the farm's sheep; daily demonstrations of sheep milking, and shearing in season, *(May-Sep)*.01323 423302

Earnley Concourse Centre,
Chichester, West Sussex:
Wide range of short courses and demonstrations covering cookery and wines; short or long weekend courses, including bakery, chocolate, Italian, Chinese and Japanese cuisines, 01243 670392

Lurgashall Watermill, Weald & Downland Open Air Museum,
Chichester, West Sussex:
The mill produces stone-ground wholemeal flour, 01243 811348

Denbies Wine Estate,
Dorking, Surrey: England's largest vineyard ; see an audio-visual introduction to the seasonal work of the estate, followed by a tour by mini-train through the winery; tasting of 3 Denbies wines in the cellars, 01306 742002

Squires Kitchen International School of Sugarcraft, *Farnham, Surrey:*
A full and regular programme of sugarcraft courses, 01252 734309

Eglantine School of Cookery,
Tunbridge Wells, Kent:
Evening and one-day courses offered covering a wide range of culinary skills, 01892 524957

Sandhurst Vineyards,
Hoads Farm, Sandhurst:
Vineyards form part of a working farm which also includes an oast house; self-guided tours of the oast during the hop-picking season, 01580 850296

Seasalter Shellfish,
Whitstable, Kent:
The story of Kent's traditional oyster and fishing industry housed in the oldest building in the harbour area, where oysters and clams can be purchased; artefacts, touch pool and video, 01227 272003

Syndale Valley Vineyards and Lavender Garden,
Faversham, Kent:
Stroll around the orchards, vineyards and lavender gardens; guided tours with tastings available for groups, 01795 890711

Local events:

April:
Farnham BeerEx 2000,
Apr 13-15 Farnham's 24th annual beer festival, 01252 726234
Bread & Yeast Cookery Workshop, *Apr 14-16* Earnley, Chichester, W Sussex - Weekend course, 01243 670392

May:
Festival of English Food & Wine, *May 13-14* Leeds Castle, Maidstone, Kent, 01622 76540014
Surrey County Show,
Guildford, 01483 414651

June:
South of England Agricultural Show, *Jun 3* Haywards Heath, West Sussex 01243 4322711
Soft Fruit Cookery Day,
Brogdale Horticultural Trust, Kent, 01795 53528630

July:
Hastings Beer & Music Festival, *Jul 6-9* Hastings, East Sussex 01424 7810668
Whitstable Oyster Festival,
Jul 30 Whitstable, Kent, Famous festival, 01227 265666

August:
Roman Food & Drink, *Aug 4-6* Dover, 01304 21010112
Chilli Fiesta, Chichester, West Sussex - Over 100 varieties of chilli peppers, cookery demonstrations, tastings and other activities, 01243 81820920

September:
Faversham Hop Festival,
Sep 1-3 Faversham, Kent, 01795 585601
Totally Tomato Show,
Sep 4-5 Chichester, W Sussex, 01243 8182099

October:
Apple Celebration, *Oct 20-22* Brogdale Horticultural Trust, Faversham, Brogdale's biggest event of the year, 01795 535286

A RATHER FINE OFFER FROM HERITAGE HOTELS

A subtle blend of red fruit
and spice with an attractive
aromatic palate,
Chateau d'Aigueville
is available for purchase
in every hotel bedroom or
on our restaurant
wine lists
at £7.95 a bottle.

Heritage Hotels – Driving Tours

Welcome to Heritage's Driving Tours, which have been designed to make your trip both relaxing and rewarding

On the following pages, we have made some suggestions as to areas you may wish to visit. Our Daily Suggested Itinerary points out highlights for the area, including places you may want to visit that are nearby, but not in the centre of town.

You may wish to design your own tour, based around a particular interest - such as cathedrals, gardens or historic houses. Simply choose the Heritage Hotels you would like to visit, and consult our reservations team on (0)345 543 555 to book your trip.

For more information contact: (0)345 543 555

Heritage Hotels – The Royal Tie

7 Day, 6 Night tour, Ascot – Winchester – Windsor

For more information contact: (0)345 543 555

Day 1 **Ascot**

Begin your driving tour in Berkshire, where society goes to the races in grand style for four days every June at Royal Ascot, and outrageous hats are the height of fashion.

- Check into the Berystede Hotel.
- Visit Ascot's racetrack (where meetings take place regularly throughout the year).
- Dine in the Hyperion Restaurant.

Day 2 **Winchester**

Winchester, the ancient capital of King Arthur's Wessex is a historic city where legend, fable and fact coinincide, and where England's royal heritage began.

- Check into The Wessex, overlooking the Cathedral.
- Take a guided tour to introduce youself to this ancient city.
- Grab lunch at any of the many cafes and small restaurants.
- Take *'The Sunset Walk'*, a step-by-step, self-guided tour through St. Giles' Hill, The Weirs and Abbey Gardens.

Day 3 **Winchester**

- Try *'The Winchester Walk'* in the morning.
- Lunch at one of the pubs or restaurants around the Square.
- Save the afternoon for a guided tour of the cathedral.
- After the cathedral enjoy the very popular *'Keats' Walk'*.
- Enjoy a leisurely dinner.

Ascot – Winchester – Windsor

Day 4 Windsor

One of The Queen's favourite residences, Windsor Castle has recently undergone a major restoration project after being damaged by fire. The Earl and Countess of Wessex married in St George's Chapel here.

- Drive to Windsor.
- Check in at the Castle Hotel, directly across from the castle.
- Tour Windsor Castle (allow approximately 3 hours).
- Return to the Castle Hotel for tea, scones and clotted cream.
- Before dinner, enjoy walking through the streets of the old town, seeing how remarkably well-preserved the buildings are.

Day 5 Windsor

- Tour the famous Eton College, founded in 1440.
- Lunch in town.
- Walk through the old town of Windsor, noting the number of lovely 16th-18th century timber-framed houses.
- Explore various antique shops or the Royal Station Arcade.
- Enjoy a drink in The Castle Hotel before dinner.

Day 6 Windsor

- Explore Windsor Great Park, and visit Frogmore House where Queen Victoria and Prince Albert are buried.
- Visit Legoland, or do some last minute shopping.
- Treat yourself to a farewell dinner at The Castle Restaurant.

Day 7 Windsor

- Return home.

Heritage Hotels – Literary Tour

5 Day, 4 Night tour, Stratford – Oxford – Marlow

For more information contact: (0)345 543 555

Day 1 **Stratford-upon-Avon**

Although Stratford-upon-Avon dates back to the Romans, today
it resembles a Tudor market town. The world of Shakespeare is
apparent everywhere, with a number of attractions all around
the town celebrating his life and works. The Other Place, the
Royal Shakespeare and The Swan theatres offer nightly
performances, and this is the provincial home of the Royal
Shakespeare Company.

- Check into The Alveston Manor.
- Stroll across the foot bridge spanning the river Avon, and
  catch a bus to tour this historic town.
- After the bus tour, return to the hotel and dine early before
  going to the theatre. Dessert can be served after the
  performance, if you desire.

Day 2 **Stratford-upon-Avon**

- After breakfast, visit Anne Hathaway's cottage, the Cage or
  Nash's House, where Shakespeare died.
- Have a late morning tea, then drive to Warwick Castle, an
  impressive medieval fortress, some 20 miles away.
- Enjoy a leisurely evening meal, and drinks in the bar.

Day 3 **Oxford**

Since the 12th century Oxford has attracted scholars, writers
and thinkers. Dorothy L. Sayers graduated from college here,

Stratford – Oxford – Marlow

P.D. James still lives in town, and Colin Dexter wrote his *Inspector Morse* novels here. Drive to Oxford, then abandon your car for the day, and explore this glorious city on foot.

- Check in at The Randolph, and take a guided walking tour of the town.
- Have lunch at Cafe Boheme, opposite Magdalen College.
- Climb the Carfax Tower for a splendid view of Oxford.
- Visit the Bodleian Library.

Day 4 Marlow

Marlow is a small village on the Thames, with lovely river walks, tempting antique shops and chic boutiques.

- After breakfast at The Randolph, take in the Ashmolean Museum or visit some of the other Oxford colleges.
- Leave for Marlow at about 2 pm, and enjoy a cream tea on arrival.
- Stroll over the famous suspension bridge into town, then dine in the hotel's gourmet restaurant overlooking the Thames.
- Pack and have a leisurely dinner.

Day 5 Marlow

- Return home.

Heritage Hotels – The Lakes

6 Day, 5 Night tour, Windermere – Ullswater

**For more information contact: (0)345 543 555
or visit www.heritage-hotels.com**

Day 1 **Windermere**

The Lake District is probably the most beautiful part of
Britain. The lakes themselves, together with the surrounding
parkland, are protected areas for bird and animal wildlife - and
the particularly British charm of the winding roads and stone
cottages is perhaps the image of Britain that many of us
still cherish.

- Check into The Old England Hotel, and admire the views
  across England's largest lake.
- Stroll through this bustling little town, and look into the
  Steamboat Museum.
- Take a cocktail in the bar before enjoying dinner in
  The Old England's restaurant.

Day 2 **Windermere**

After a hearty breakfast, a must for *Peter Rabbit* fans is a drive to
Hill Top, Beatrix Potter's house, which is now a museum.

- As an alternative, take a cruise on the lake.
- Drive to Grasmere, check into The Swan and enjoy dinner
  in the restaurant.

Day 3 **Grasmere**

- Dove Cottage, home to William Wordsworth and his sister
  Dorothy, is well worth a visit and within easy reach of
  the hotel.

- Grasmere gingerbread is delicious, so buy some in the village and it will keep you going as you take a walk around the lake.
- Return to the hotel for a cream tea, and then read or walk along the lake until dinner time.

Day 4 **Ullswater**

After breakfast, drive to Leeming House at Ullswater. This gracious hotel was once a private residence and is surrounded by 20 acres of landscaped gardens.

- For confident hikers, Helvellyn is a climb which well repays the effort, as there are tremendous views of the region from its peak.
- Relax in one of the lounges before treating yourself to a well-earned dinner in The Lake District Restaurant of the Year, The Regency Restaurant.

Day 5 **Ullswater**

- Enjoy a lengthy breakfast, then meander through The Tree Trail – half a mile of woodland with trees from all over the world.
- Drive to Penrith for a spot of lunch and some shopping
- Enjoy a few drinks at the bar before another fine meal.

Day 6 **Ullswater**

- Return home.

Join one of the most
generous
hotel rewards
programmes in the world

Join our generous new rewards programme and collect MOMENTS points at Heritage and other Forte hotels worldwide. Redeem your points for free nights and other valuable rewards. Enjoy recognition as one of our loyal guests and receive special offers of direct interest to you. It only takes a moment to become a member - so get on the line today.

❧ MOMENTS.COM

visit www.moments.com or phone 0800 500 500

   _Le_ MERIDIEN   HERITAGE HOTELS   Posthouse

Divisions of the Forte Hotel Group

Heritage Hotels – Music at Leisure

The world's greatest music in exquisite surroundings

**For more information contact: (0)345 543 555
or visit www.heritage-hotels.com**

Music at Leisure
weekends from
£259 per person

What's included:
- 2 recitals including
  programmes, champagne
  reception – Friday and
  Saturday evenings
- 2 nights' accommodation
  sharing a twin/double room
  with private bathroom (or
  single room) full traditional
  breakfast every morning
- 3 course evening meal
  with coffee
- Saturday morning event

An unrivalled opportunity for music-lovers to enjoy some of the world's greatest music, performed in convivial surroundings by some of the world's finest musicians. This year's exciting programme of recitals takes place in hotels as varied as the inspiring musical schedule itself, with each venue being renowned for its historic charm and relaxed ambience.

Kathryn Stott

Each evening on these house-party weekends begins with a black-tie champagne reception before the recital and ends with the musicians joining the guests for dinner. The Director of Music at Leisure is Leonard Pearcey, who writes:

"We close our 35th Season with The Dante String Quartet in the period surroundings of Stratford's Alveston Manor offering 'Visions of Italy' on the Friday and Stravinsky, Mozart and Sibelius on the Saturday; and with a special Gala weekend to celebrate the reopening after extensive refurbishment of The Swan at Lavenham, the home of Music at Leisure, where our special guests are The Schidlof String Quartet.

"Our 36th Season is launched in the elegance of Cheltenham's Queen's Hotel, where Melvyn Tan's fortepiano brings us an all-Mozart programme and then combines Beethoven and Schubert. Two weeks later pianist Leon McCawley adds Schumann and Chopin to Melvyn's mix against the magnificent backdrop of the Peak District; and a fortnight after that in Canterbury The Allegri String Quartet feature Lombardini, Dvorak, Beethoven, Haydn, Borodin and Schubert.

"I first heard The Yggdrasil String Quartet at the City of London Festival and immediately invited them to appear at Brandon Hall; they include Haydn's 'Lark', Beethoven's 'Harp' and Dvorak's 'American'. Pianist Kathryn Stott has delighted Music at Leisure audiences many times before; on this occasion The White Hart at Salisbury will echo to the music of eleven different composers with strong French, Scandinavian and Spanish influences.

Yggdrasil String Quartet

"We reach our Christmas and New Year break back at The Swan at Lavenham, with the exciting combination of Jeremy Menuhin and The Haffner Wind Quintet. Full details of the actual programmes to be played at each weekend appear in 'Prelude', the newsletter for The Friends of Music at Leisure. It costs nothing to join, so if you would like to receive the newsletter, please write to: The Friends of Music at Leisure (HTG), 53 Queens Road, Wimbledon, London SW19 8NP.

"All in all, you will find it a very special way to enjoy music, at leisure."

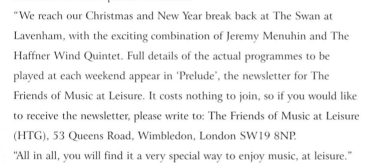

Music at Leisure Calendar of Events						
Date	Hotel Name	Location	Musicians	Price per person	Telephone	Page
Apr 7, 8	The Alveston Manor	Stratford	Dante String Quartet	£289	(0)870 400 8181	130
May 19, 20	The Swan FULL	Lavenham	Schidlof String Quartet	£259	(0)870 400 8116	98
Sep 22, 23	The Queen's	Cheltenham	Melvyn Tan, fortepiano	£275	(0)870 400 8107	66
Sep 29, 30	The New Bath Hotel	Matlock Bath	Leon McCawley, piano	£275	(0)870 400 8119	106
Oct 13, 14	The Chaucer Hotel	Canterbury	Allegri String Quartet	£265	(0)870 400 8106	64
Oct 27, 28	Brandon Hall	Coventry	Yggdrasil String Quartet	£259	(0)870 400 8105	70
Nov 17, 18	The White Hart	Salisbury	Kathryn Stott, piano	£265	(0)870 400 8125	126
Dec 1, 2	The Swan	Lavenham	Jeremy Menuhin, piano and The Haffner Wind Quintet	£289	(0)870 400 8116	98

Heritage Hotels – Break for Murder

Joy Swift's Original Murder Weekends

**For more information contact: (0)345 543 555
or visit www.heritage-hotels.com**

Break for Murder
weekends from
£190 per person

What's included:
- welcome reception
- 2 nights' accommodation including dinner and full traditional breakfast – sharing a twin or double room, with colour TV
- tea and coffee-making facilities, phone, private en suite bathroom
- Saturday lunch
- full 'Break for Murder' programme with competitions, games and actors

Imagine enjoying dinner, then a stranger dies dramatically at your table. Who was he? Why was he killed and, most importantly, by whom?

Joy Swift's Original Murder Weekends, now in their highly successful 20th year, guarantee realism, shocking excitement and fun.

You will arrive on Friday evening, check in and be welcomed to a cocktail reception at 8 pm, followed by a sumptuous dinner.

During the evening a murder will be committed. The police will arrive and begin their investigations. This is the moment for you to become a sleuth.

After breakfast on Saturday, the police will set up an Incident Room, where vital evidence will be exhibited. You will be free to enjoy the surrounding area or pursue your enquiries!

(Even if you meet the actors at the local shops, you can still question them, as they will stay in character all weekend.)
After lunch there will be more ghastly goings-on and devilish deeds. On Saturday night there will be a themed party with dinner, dancing and death!
(In true style, there is never just one murder!)

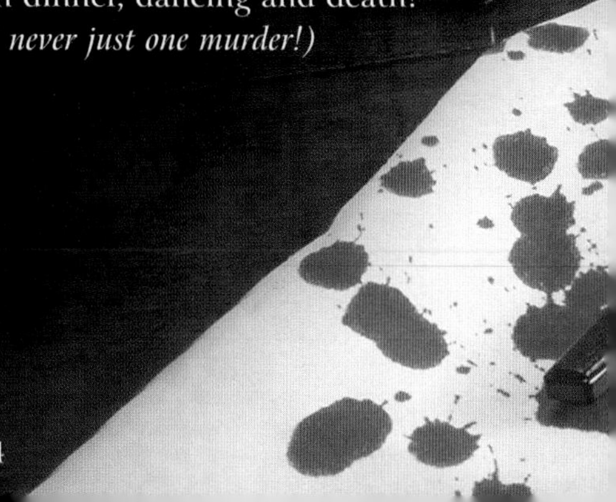

"I can't tell you how much I enjoy the cerebral challenge your weekends pose and can only say I hope you never, ever run out of ideas."

Mrs Barnes,
Boxworth, Cambs

"The weekend was packed with action, without a dull moment. The quality of the acting and the plot made it an amazing weekend. The fancy dress and games were thoroughly enjoyable. We loved every minute... Thank you, I'll definitely be back and recommend you to everyone."

Mrs Blake,
Redditch, Worcs

POISON

Heritage Hotels – Break for Murder

Joy Swift's Original Murder Weekends

**For more information contact: (0)345 543 555
or visit www.heritage-hotels.com**

"Well, everything went swimmingly – great hotel, great food and great to see the old gang again – that is, until the very last moment. Then Margaret solved the crime! Not only that, she was awarded a damn' certificate to prove it! Now, she does nothing but sit watching all the detective programmes on TV. And – you might guess – every time she solves another mystery, I get the certificate waved in my face!"

*Mr & Mrs V. Garvey,
Tunbridge Wells, Kent*

On Sunday morning everyone is gathered by the Inspector, who explains his suspects' motives, points out key clues and ultimately reveals the murderer.
Will you be able to nail the murderer too? If so, you could win one of our coveted trophies.
It will be a weekend you will always remember – so why not have a stab at it?

The Scenes of the Crimes

Date	Hotel Name	Location	Price per person	Page
Mar 31 - Apr 2	Brandon Hall	Brandon near Coventry	£195	70
Mar 31 - Apr 2	The Bush	Farnham	£199	84
Apr 7-9	The Black Swan	Helmsley	£205	88
Apr 14-16	Frimley Hall	Camberley	£199	62
Apr 21-23	The Berystede	Ascot	£199	50
Apr 28-30	The Old England	Bowness on Windermere	£195	142
May 5-7	The Wessex	Winchester	£199	140
May 12-14	The Old England	Bowness on Windermere	£195	142
May 19-21	The Berystede	Ascot	£199	50
May 26-28	The Chaucer	Canterbury	£195	64
Jul 21-23	The Burford Bridge	Box Hill	£199	58
Aug 4-6	Whately Hall	Banbury	£195	52
Aug 25-27	The Berystede	Ascot	£199	50
Sep 22-24	The Avonmouth	Mudeford	£195	108
Sep 29 - 1 Oct	Brandon Hall	Brandon near Coventry	£195	70
Oct 6-8	Whately Hall	Banbury	£195	52
Oct 13-15	Frimley Hall	Camberley	£199	62
Oct 20-22	The Burford Bridge	Box Hill	£199	58
Oct 27-29	The Old England	Bowness on Windermere	£199	142
Oct 27-29	The Berystede	Ascot	£199	50
Nov 3-5	The Bush	Farnham	£199	84
Nov 10-12	The White Hart	Salisbury	£199	126
Nov 10-12	The Black Swan	Helmsley	£205	88
Nov 17-19	Alveston Manor	Stratford upon Avon	£205	130
Nov 24-26	The Berystede	Ascot	£199	50
Dec 1-3	The Francis	Bath	£210	56
Dec 30 - Jan 1	Whately Hall	Banbury	£230	52

Heritage Hotels – A Sporting Offer

Liven up your special break with a little extra activity

**For more information contact: (0)870 400 8855
or visit www.heritage-hotels.com**

For those of you who like their Leisure Breaks livened up with a little extra recreational activity, Heritage Hotels have got the very thing: A Sporting Offer. Whether your taste is for a round of golf, riding *(or having a flutter whilst somebody else sits on the horse)*, motor racing, shooting or archery, rock climbing, a range of water sports or even ballooning, we have a hotel in most parts of the country that can organise a special break for you.

Pg.	Location	Hotel	G	WS	F	S/A	O	H
50	Ascot	The Berystede	•			•	•	•
52	Banbury	Whately Hall			•	•	•	
54	Bath	The Bath Spa Hotel	•		•	•	•	•
56	Bath	The Francis	•		•		•	•
62	Camberley	Frimley Hall	•			•	•	•
64	Canterbury	The Chaucer Hotel	•	•				
66	Cheltenham	The Queen's						•
70	Coventry	Brandon Hall	•		•	•	•	
72	Dartmouth	The Dart Marina	•	•				
76	Dovedale	Peveril of the Peak				•	•	
86	Grasmere	The Swan	•					•
104	Marlow	The Compleat Angler	•		•	•	•	•
106	Matlock Bath	The New Bath Hotel			•	•	•	
110	North Berwick	The Marine	•			•	•	
124	St Andrews	Rusacks Hotel	•			•	•	
126	Salisbury	The White Hart	•			•	•	•
130	Stratford-upon-Avon	The Alveston Manor	•			•		
138	Ullswater	Leeming House	•	•		•	•	•
140	Winchester	The Wessex	•			•	•	•
142	Windermere	The Old England	•	•		•	•	
146	Woodstock	The Bear	•			•	•	

G Golf
WS Water Sports
F Flying
S/A Shooting/Archery
O Outdoor
H Horseracing

Heritage Hotels – the Festive Season

Truly memorable Christmas or New Year celebrations

**For more information contact: (0)870 400 8855
or visit www.heritage-hotels.com**

Our tailor-made festive breaks not only offer the perfect blend of customary Heritage hospitality and exemplary service, but also an exciting choice of packages and entertainment that cater for all. So relax, and leave all the usual holiday hassles far behind.

Traditional Christmas

Comprehensive Package includes:

• 3 nights' accommodation 24-26 December, • Welcome reception on Christmas Eve • Full traditional breakfast each morning • Minimum 3-course dinner or buffet each evening • Morning coffee & afternoon tea each day • Welcome drink on return from Midnight Mass • Traditional 4-course lunch on Christmas Day • Visit from Santa Claus on Christmas Day • Local entertainment, such as bell ringers, pantomime, carol singers • Details of local places of interest open during the period • Boxing Day buffet or 3-course lunch • Boxing Day 3-course dinner and entertainment

Peace & Quiet Christmas

Comprehensive Package includes:

• 3 nights' accommodation 24-26 December • Welcome reception on Christmas Eve • Full traditional breakfast each morning • Minimum 3-course dinner or buffet each evening • Morning coffee & afternoon tea each day • Traditional 4-course lunch on Christmas Day • Introduction to local places of interest open during the period • Boxing Day buffet or 3-course lunch • Boxing Day 3-course dinner

New Year Celebration

Welcome 2001 in champagne style. Join us in a New Year Celebration in one of our ideally placed hotels up and down the country. We'll lay on everything you could possibly need, so all you have to do is relax and enjoy the time of your life along

Christmas and New Year Packages

with your family, partner or friends. It's the perfect way to see in the New Year

Comprehensive Package includes:

Accommodation • Champagne Reception • New Year's Eve Dinner • Traditional celebrations at midnight • Fireworks at selected hotels • Full traditional breakfast

For a copy of our Christmas & New Year Celebrations brochure call (0)345 700 350 quoting 'HCNY'.

Visiting Friends & Relatives

If you're planning a pre- or post-holiday visit to friends or relatives, there's a conveniently located Heritage Hotel just waiting to welcome you. Our special 'friends and relatives' rates include accommodation and full traditional breakfast and are available only on the following dates:

17-23 December 2000 • 27-29 December 2000

02-09 January 2001

4 CHANNEL ABS,

COMBINED AUTOMATIC AND TRANSFER GEARBOX,

5 SUSPENSION SETTINGS

AND GREAT BIG COMFY SEATS.

If Range Rover was only the best 4x4 in the world for supermodels,

it wouldn't be the best.

RANGE ROVER

Heritage Hotels – Abingdon

The Upper Reaches

Thames Street, Abingdon, Oxfordshire OX14 3JA *See map page 4*
Tel: (0)870 400 8101 Fax: (0)123 555 5182 General Manager: Daniel Loosley
E-mail: HeritageHotels_Abingdon.Upper_Reaches@forte-hotels.com
Reservations: (0)870 400 8855 www.heritage-hotels.com

How to get there:

Upon reaching the town centre, turn from Stratton Way into Stert Street (the A415). Those arriving by boat should be able to make their own navigational arrangements.

Facilities: 31 bedrooms, some with river views, 1 four-poster, 9 half-testers, hairdryer, trouser press, restaurant, bar, 2 lounges, river mooring, fresh water fishing, free swimming in nearby leisure centre *(30 second walk)*, free car park.

Family: Baby listening, baby sitting.

Leisure rates pppn

Midweek:	BB	DBB
Apr–Jun 2000	£ 70	£ 85
Jul–Aug	£ 60	£ 75
Sep–Nov	£ 70	£ 85
Dec–Feb	£ 60	£ 75
March 2001	£ 70	£ 85
Weekend:	BB	DBB
Apr–Aug 2000	£ 67	£ 82
Sep–Feb	£ 56	£ 71
March 2001	£ 67	£ 82

Riverview Break rates

Validity dates: all dates until March 2001
Weekends: May–September, £240 per person for two nights
October–April, £220 per person for two nights
Based on two people sharing.
Please quote 'Special Break' when booking.

A tranquil location on an island in the Thames. This small 31-bedroom hotel, which is built from a converted corn mill is only a minute walk from the delightful and historic town of Abingdon. Arrive by boat to dock in private moorings. Some rooms overlook the Thames, and the Millwheel Restaurant *(so called because of the existing millwheel in the dining room)* has a traditional menu.

Riverview Break:

Arrive on Friday evening at the Upper Reaches and check into your room overlooking the River Thames. There will be flowers and champagne to greet you. Then head down to the Millwheel Restaurant for a three-course meal. Following breakfast the next morning you can travel to Oxford, which is only a 15-minute drive. There a tour of the Oxford Story attraction has been arranged, and you will be transported through the story of the university over the centuries. While in Oxford you may wish to visit the colleges, and afternoon tea has been organised at the famous Randolph Hotel for you before you return to Abingdon. No doubt, after such a busy day you will want to relax and the Millwheel Restaurant is again the setting for your evening meal. Perhaps after breakfast on Sunday you would like to stroll along the riverbank or just sit and watch the boats go by before departing.

What's included in your break:
- 2 nights' dinner, bed and breakfast
- champagne and flowers in your room on arrival
- 3-course dinner in the restaurant each night *(wine not included in price)*
- full English breakfast both days
- entry to the Oxford Story attraction *(Oxford 15 minutes' drive)*
- afternoon tea at the Randolph Hotel, Oxford

Abingdon – Oxfordshire

1 Morland Brewery

The sweet smell of beer brewing wafts through the town from here, the country's second oldest independent brewery. In 1927, the production of an unusual MG saloon became the inspiration for its famous strong pale ale 'Old Speckled Hen' and the MG Car Club now organises regular rallies from here.

2 Dorchester on Thames

This old Roman town is dominated by its 12th century abbey, which includes the famous Jesse Window, added to the church in the 14th century. The town's many antiques shops are its other main charm.

Dorchester on Thames with the abbey in the background.

3 Wittenham Clumps

The game of Poohsticks, when people throw sticks over a bridge into the flow of the water and compete to see which stick emerges first on the other side of the bridge, was immortalised in A.A. Milne's Winnie the Pooh stories.

4 Didcot Railway Centre

This museum re-creates the golden age of the Great Western Railway, with steam locomotives, broad gauge railway, and a display of relics. Steam trains run daily April to September. *(Weekends only all other times)*

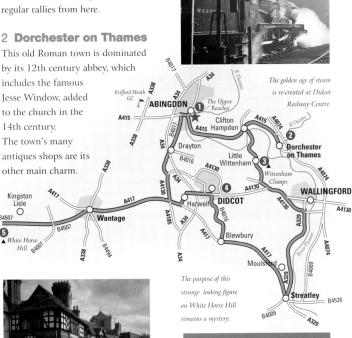

The golden age of steam is re-created at Didcot Railway Centre.

The purpose of this strange looking figure on White Horse Hill remains a mystery.

5 White Horse Hill

This 375ft shape of a horse is thought to have been carved into the chalk hills around 2000 BC. Its meaning is unclear, although some believe it to be an ancient form of signposting.

Local attractions/events:

Open all year (except some public holidays) unless otherwise shown

Abingdon:

Museum: local archaeology, exhibitions and crafts
Thames Bridge: a starting point to explore the many historic ruins of England's oldest town
Morris Dancing: this dates from 1560 and can be regularly seen in the Market Place
Crafts Festival: mid-October – an ideal opportunity to shop for Christmas gifts!

Surrounding areas:

(also refer to pages 115/117 & 147)

Sutton Courtenay: an idyllic village, just a short walk along the Thames Path
Pendon Museum, *Long Wittenham:* reproduces, in miniature, the 1930s English countryside (weekends only Jan-Nov)
Wallingford: this historic town with a medieval bridge, Castle and Gardens is perfectly captured in its local museum, which houses many artefacts from the past
Wyld Court Rainforest, *Hampstead Norreys:* unique conservation project under 20,000 sq ft of glass
Mill Gallery, *Goring:* art and crafts by local artists, located in a beautiful riverside village
Lambourn Racehorse Trainers: a rare insight into the world of horseracing, with guided tours of the stables
Ashdown House, *nr Astbury:* unusual 17th century mansion with fine views (Mar-Oct)
The Maize Maze, *Frilford:* get lost in a giant maze created from 2m high forage maize in the shape of a pirate ship – and when you finally find your way out, visit Millet's Farm Shop
The Holies and Lardon Chase, *nr Goring:* beautiful woodland and downland walks on the hillside overlooking Goring and the Thames Valley

Heritage Hotels – Alfriston

The Star Inn

Alfriston, Nr Polegate, East Sussex BN26 5TH *See map page 5*
Tel: (0)870 400 8102 Fax: (0)132 387 0922 General Manager: Graham Hawksworth
E-mail: HeritageHotels_Alfriston. Star_Inn@forte-hotels.com
Reservations: (0)870 400 8855 www.heritage-hotels.com

How to get there:
Alfriston is situated off
the A27, near Polegate,
East Sussex. The Star Inn
lies at its heart.

Facilities: 37 bedrooms,
3 feature rooms, hairdryer,
trouser press, restaurant,
bar, 2 lounges, open fires in
winter, local leisure facilities,
free car park.
Family: Baby listening,
baby sitting (on request).

Leisure rates pppn

Midweek:	BB	DBB
Apr 2000	£ 48	£ 63
May–Jun	£ 50	£ 65
Jul–Nov	£ 55	£ 70
Dec–Feb	£ 45	£ 60
March 2001	£ 50	£ 65
Weekend:	BB	DBB
Apr 2000	£ 53	£ 68
May–Nov	£ 66	£ 80
Dec–Feb	£ 49	£ 64
March 2001	£ 66	£ 80

Special Break rates

Validity dates: all dates until
March 2001
Star Inn all-inclusive stay
3 nights and for only an extra
£10 per person per night *(on
top of the leisure break rate)*
we will include morning coffee,
lunch, afternoon tea, draught
beer, house wine and soft drinks
***Please quote 'Special Break'
when booking.***

Prince Edward is among the guests who have visited this famous
14th-century inn, which was once a renowned meeting place for
smugglers in times gone by. Oak beams and open log fires offer mellow
reminders of the past and create an intimate atmosphere in the bar.
Set in the South Downs, there are many fine walks, and the famous
South Downs Way starts right at the door of the inn. Take in the
16-foot square church at Lullington. Local leisure facilities – pool, sauna,
tennis, gym, horse-riding and golf course.

All Inclusive Break:

The Star Inn is the perfect gateway to the South
Downs, set in the traditional Sussex village of
Alfriston. The village is just a stroll away from the
Clergy House, the first National Trust property;
together with the Long Man and the White Horse
chalk carvings you can get a taste for the history
of the region. Beachy Head, the Seven Sisters,
the Cuckmere Valley and the Meanders at Exceat
are some of the natural features – all within walking
distance – that make this area so special.
For the fit, the South Downs Way passes the
doorstep for walking, mountain biking, paragliding
and breathtaking views.

Alfriston – East Sussex

1 English Wine Centre, Alfriston

Southern England has been home to the English wine industry since Roman times. The wine centre in Alfriston includes a museum explaining the production, with tastings of a range of award-winning wines. Staff also offer information on visiting other vineyards in the area.

Old cottages line the main street at Alfriston.

2 Charleston Farmhouse

During the early 20th century, this farmhouse was the meeting place of the group of English artists and writers known as the Bloomsbury Set. The house and gardens have been preserved as they were in their heyday.

3 Glyndebourne

Founded in 1938, Glyndebourne is an independent opera venue and a highlight for many on the summer calendar. It is known as much for its spectacular productions, often daring in their choice of programme, as it is for the extravagant picnics enjoyed by opera buffs in its grounds.

4 Bluebell Railway Museum

This nine-mile steam railway route north to Kingscote is a perennial favourite with both adults and children alike. The name stems from the woodlands filled with bluebells along the route. *(Trains run weekends only)*

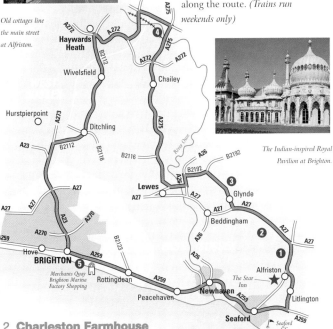

The Indian-inspired Royal Pavilion at Brighton.

5 Brighton

This seaside resort in many ways epitomises English holiday-making, with its ice cream sellers, deckchairs and pier. Do visit the Royal Pavilion and the charming shopping area known as "The Lanes".

Local attractions/events:

Open all year (except some public holidays) unless otherwise shown

Alfriston:

Clergy House: a 14th century thatched house, where you can discover why the chalk floor is covered with sour milk! *(Mar-Oct)*
Drusillas Park: described as 'the best small zoo in the country'

Surrounding areas:

Mickleham Priory, nr Hailsham: a tranquil island setting surrounded by England's longest water-filled medieval moat *(Mar-Oct)*
Bentley Wildfowl & Motor Museum, Halland: with more than 2,000 waterfowl, over 100 vehicles and a unique collection of waterfowl paintings *(Mar-Oct)*
Barkham Manor Vineyard, nr Uckfield: the most visually impressive vineyard in the country
Pooh Corner, Hartfield: the largest collection of 'Pooh-phernalia'
Wakehurst Place, Ardingly: exotic gardens and native woodland surround a 16th century mansion
Sheffield Park Garden, nr Haywards Heath: lakes and waterfalls laid out by 'Capability' Brown *(Mar-Dec)*
Nynam Gardens, nr Haywards Heath: romantic garden with rare plants from around the world *(Mar-Oct)*
Borde Hill Gardens, Haywards Heath: voted 'Visitor Attraction of the Year 1999'
Monk's House, nr Lewes: the writer Virginia Woolf lived here between 1919-1941 *(Mar-Oct)*
Plumpton & Brighton Races: 'flutter' the day away at either course
Paradise Park, Newhaven: dinosaurs, Sussex in miniature, water gardens and much more!
Pevensey Castle: discover 2000 years of history in the battlements, towers, dungeons and castle ruins
Herstmonceux Castle, Hailsham: 15th century moated castle in 300 acres of glorious woodland and gardens *(Apr-Oct)*

Heritage Hotels – Amersham

The Crown

16 High Street, Amersham, Buckinghamshire HP7 0DH *See map page 4*
Tel: (0)870 400 8103 Fax: (0)149 443 1283
E-mail: HeritageHotels_Amersham.Crown@forte-hotels.com
Reservations: (0)870 400 8855 www.heritage-hotels.com

How to get there:

To reach the Crown, take the A413 London Road into Old Amersham. Turn left into the High Street and you will see the hotel ahead on the left. Parking to rear of hotel via Whielden Street.

Facilities: 19 bedrooms, 2 four-poster mini-suites, 2 twin suites, hairdryer, trouser press, restaurant, bar, lounge, open fires in winter, free car park.
Family: Baby listening facilities.

Leisure rates pppn

Midweek:	BB	DBB
Apr–Mar 2001	£ 85	£105
Weekend:	BB	DBB
Apr–Jun 2000	£ 55	£ 70
Jul–Nov	£ 58	£ 73
Dec–Feb	£ 53	£ 68
March 2001	£ 55	£ 70

Special Break rates

June–October
Ski clinic
£200 per person for two nights
Snowboarding clinic
£219 per person for two nights
November–May
Ski clinic
£190 per person for two nights
Snowboarding clinic
£205 per person for two nights
Please quote 'Special Break' when booking.

This glorious old coaching inn added further sheen to its glowing reputation when it made an appearance in *Four Weddings and a Funeral* with Hugh Grant and Andie MacDowell. Full timber beams, open log fires and the candlelit Courtyard Restaurant reflect the authentic Elizabethan atmosphere, and intricate hand-painted murals original to the period are miraculously preserved along with the traditional decor of the four-poster suites.

Ski or Snowboarding Break:

Visit old Amersham, a gem of England's past. Enjoy an opportunity to combine the thrill of a day's skiing or snowboarding in a forest setting with the romantic character of this 15th-century inn, as featured in the film *Four Weddings and a Funeral*.
Explore Old Amersham, which abounds in antique shops and fashionable boutiques, and return to the Crown for a scrumptious afternoon cream tea in the Elizabethan lounge.
Waiting in your room will be a chilled bottle of champagne, an ideal aperitif to a three-course candlelit dinner with coffee in the Courtyard Restaurant. Round off the evening with a nightcap by a roaring fire.
Enjoy a leisurely breakfast before setting out for the

Summit Ski Centre near Wycombe for a fun-packed day.
Having spent an exciting day on the slopes, retire to the bar for the après-ski followed by a candlelit dinner. Refreshed, tuck into a leisurely breakfast then, prior to winding your way home, visit picturesque Marlow on Thames for a riverside stroll.

What's included in your break:
• 2 nights' dinner, bed and breakfast
• a bottle of champagne on arrival in your room on the first night
• a day's clinic in skiing or snowboarding inclusive of refreshments, lunch and equipment hire
• afternoon tea on the day of arrival

Amersham – Buckinghamshire

1 Amersham Old Town and Museum

Half timbered buildings, picturesque cottages and a wonderful selection of exclusive designer and craft shops surround the award winning Museum. Exhibits include archaeological finds from many aspects of local life, as well as the town's WWII involvement with barrage balloon making. There is a plentiful supply of restaurants and coaching inns, notably the Kings Arms, also used as a location in the film *Four Weddings and a Funeral*.

An attraction of the Old Town Heritage Day is the horse drawn coach rides.

2 Chiltern Open Air Museum

Step back in time at this venue with demonstrations of living history, traditional skills and hands-on activities. Get a feel for the *Forties* in the fully furnished Prefab building or visit the Victorian Toll House. Experience 50 AD at the Iron Age House and explore many other historic buildings re-erected in a relaxing countryside setting.

3 Jordans

A popular village with visitors from the USA, the 17th century farmhouse was once home to the Quakers. The Mayflower Barn is reputedly built with the timbers of the boat which carried the Pilgrim Fathers in 1620. Outside the Meeting House is the graveyard of William Penn, founder of Pennsylvania.

4 St Albans

One of the first Roman towns to be established in England, St Albans thrived over the centuries. It has a Norman Cathedral dating from 1077.

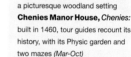

St. Albans' cathedral includes the tomb of the city's patron saint.

5 Woburn Abbey

Not in fact an Abbey, but a house, Woburn was built in the 18th century on the site of a former church. Inside is a priceless art collection, with works by Rembrandt.

Heritage Hotels – Ascot

The Berystede

Bagshot Road, Sunninghill, Ascot, Berkshire SL5 9JH *See map page 4*
Tel: (0)870 400 8111 Fax: (0)134 487 3061 General Manager: Brian Shanahan
E-mail: HeritageHotels_Ascot.Berystede@forte-hotels.com
Reservations: (0)870 400 8855 www.heritage-hotels.com

How to get there:

The Berystede Hotel is on Bagshot Road, about four miles from junction 3 of the M3. Those who prefer to avoid the dubious pleasures of the motorway can reach the hotel from the A329, approximately one mile along the B3020.

Facilities: 78 bedrooms,

6 family rooms, 3 four-posters, 4 suites, 24-hour room service, hairdryer, trouser press, satellite TV, award-winning Hyperion Restaurant, oak lounge, open fires in winter, croquet lawn, outdoor heated swimming pool *(May–September)*, putting green, free car park.
Family: Baby listening.

This old country house, set among nine acres of fine landscaped grounds, is a popular spot with golfing celebrities when playing at the Wentworth Golf Course. Try your hand at croquet on the lawn or cleave through the swimming pool before pondering the choices of the traditional English menu at Hyperion Restaurant. A favourite with sporting guests, the Diadem Bar is fashioned after a gentleman's smoking room. Later, relax in the Library Lounge *(full of intriguing hidden panels)* with its selection of books and, on chilly days, an open log fire.

Leisure rates pppn

Midweek:	BB	DBB
Apr–Mar 2001	£ 90	£110
Weekend:	BB	DBB
Apr–Mar 2001	£ 50	£ 70

Special Break rates

£200 per person for two nights.
£50 per room to upgrade to suite
Please quote 'Special Break' when booking.

Golfing Break:

A hotel since the turn of the century, the Berystede's distinctive facade – a blend of Gothic and Tudor styles – conceals a wealth of creature comforts and delights.

On arrival at the Berystede relax and enjoy afternoon tea in the Oak Lounge. Dinner will be served in the award-winning Hyperion Restaurant accompanied by a glass of wine.

Enjoy a leisurely breakfast, then on to Mill Ride for a round of golf on this championship standard course.

Another chance to dine in the Hyperion Restaurant and listen to the resident pianist awaits you. Before your departure enjoy a wholesome breakfast and perhaps pay a visit to Ascot Racecourse.

What's included in your break:
• 2 nights' dinner, bed and breakfast
• a glass of wine with dinner each
• afternoon tea on the day of your arrival
• 1 round of golf at Mill Ride Golf Club

Ascot – Berkshire

1 Ascot Racecourse

For four days each June, Ascot is taken over by the horse races known as Royal Ascot. The event is as much associated with fashion as it is with betting, with spectators dressed in haute couture style, most notably with large, often outrageous hats. The royal family are also in attendance, travelling down the course in open-top carriages. Other races take place throughout the year.

Queen Elizabeth II and the Duke of Edinburgh at Royal Ascot.

3 Basildon Park

A Palladian mansion built in the 18th century from a fortune made in the East Indies, it has recently been restored by Lord & Lady Iliffe and adorned with quality pictures and furniture. *(Mar-Oct)*

West Front, Stratfield Saye House: Home of the Dukes of Wellington.

4 Stratfield Saye House

Once home to the Duke of Wellington, the present Duke and Duchess still retain many of his belongings. Within the grounds are the American Gardens and the grave of his favourite charger, Copenhagen. The Wellington Exhibition details the life and times of the Great Duke. *(May-Sep)*

One of the many colourful vistas to be seen in Savill Garden.

2 Savill Garden

Set within the grounds of historic Windsor Great Park, Sir Eric Savill designed these gardens to be the finest woodland and botanical garden, creating harmonious colour and vista throughout the seasons.

5 Wellington Country Park

Peaceful woodland, herds of deer, other wildlife and water birds in a natural environment. Explore on foot or by boat. Nearby is Wellington Riding School, one of the country's finest equestrian centres, offering lessons for all levels of rider.

Local attractions/events:

Open all year (except some public holidays) unless otherwise shown

Surrounding areas:
(also refer to pages 63 & 145)

Wentworth Golf Course: dating from 1895, this is one of the most renowned in England and the favourite of many celebrities

Southhill Park Arts Centre, *Bracknell:* everything from Art exhibitions to music events, something is always going on here

Look Out Discovery Park, *Bracknell:* an interactive science discovery centre that brings alive the mysteries of science and nature

Windsor Great Park: ideal for summer picnics or an afternoon stroll and, within easy reach, all of the attractions that Windsor itself has to offer *(see page 145)*

Beale Park, *Lower Basildon:* this Thames-side park provides family entertainment, rare animals and a narrow gauge railway *(Feb-Dec)*

The Vyne, *nr Basingstoke:* built in the early 16th century, the house contains a fascinating Tudor chapel with Renaissance glass, a Palladian staircase and fine furniture *(Mar-Oct)*

Reading: worth a visit, and providing an opportunity to indulge in its history or yourself – with its shopping centres, cafés and restaurants

Museum and Art Gallery, *Reading:* amongst the many interesting exhibits is a copy of the Bayeux Tapestry

A Murder Mystery Weekend hotel – see pages 34-35

Heritage Hotels – Banbury

Whately Hall

Banbury Cross, Banbury, Oxfordshire OX16 0AN *See map page 4*
Tel: (0)870 400 8104 Fax: (0)129 527 1736 General Manager: Susan Lines
E-mail: HeritageHotels_Banbury.Whately_Hall@forte-hotels.com
Reservations: (0)870 400 8855 www.heritage-hotels.com

How to get there:
Whately Hall is very close to Banbury Cross itself. Follow the A422 for about a mile, heading west from junction 11 off the M40.

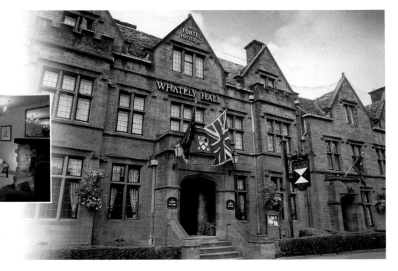

Facilities: 71 bedrooms,
5 suites, hairdryer, restaurant, bar, 2 lounges, open fires in winter, garden, croquet lawn, free car park.

The cast of Jane Austen's *Pride and Prejudice* got into character quite easily during their stay here while filming the TV series in the area. Hidden staircases, priest holes and the resident ghost of Father Bernard are famously part of the charm of this 17th-century treasure. An oak-panelled restaurant overlooking a croquet lawn serves traditional fare in a mellow atmosphere. A good starting point for exploring the Cotswolds, Stratford-upon-Avon, Warwick Castle and Oxford

Leisure rates pppn

Midweek:	BB	DBB
Apr–Jun 2000	£ 65	£ 85
Jul-Aug	£ 55	£ 75
Sept-Feb	£ 65	£ 85
March 2001	£ 70	£ 90
Weekend:	**BB**	**DBB**
Apr–Jun 2000	£ 38	£ 55
Jul-Aug	£ 35	£ 55
Sept-Feb	£ 38	£ 55
March 2001	£ 40	£ 57

Gateway to the Cotswolds rates

£135 per person for two nights
(Bonus Night: £28.50 per person)
Please quote 'Special Break' when booking.

Gateway to the Cotswolds:

Stay in the historic market town of Banbury and tour the fabulous Cotswold villages .

Day 1 – Armed with your complimentary copy of the fascinating guide to the Cotswolds written by Susan Hill and an Ordnance Survey map, you can plan your tour over a leisurely breakfast. Your welcome pack will include details of many of the main attractions of the area as well as discounts for entry into some. Enjoy lunch in one of the many fine country pubs.

Day 2 – The Cotswolds covers a large area so you may want to do some more exploring, or alternatively travel a short distance north to the magnificent medieval castle of Warwick. Complimentary entry to the castle is covered, and highlights include the grounds laid out by

'Capability' Brown through to the Royal Weekend party showing Daisy, Countess of Warwick and the 'Marlborough Set' to the mighty defences of the Ramparts and Ghost Tower.

What's included in your break:
• accommodation in a twin or double room on Friday and Saturday nights
• a three-course dinner each evening
• full English breakfast each morning
• a complimentary copy of Susan Hill's book *Spirit of the Cotswolds*
• a complimentary Ordinance Survey map of the Cotswolds
• free entrance to the castle and grounds at Warwick

Banbury – Oxfordshire

1 Banbury Museum

Chronicles the story of 'Banburyshire' and its Saxon and Medieval origins. Banbury Cross *(of Nursery Rhyme fame)* is just one of the features of the historic trail, which includes cheese, ale, plush cloth and, of course, the famous eponymous cakes.

2 Broughton Castle

This 14th century castle, with its attractive moat, was restored in the late 16th century and has many fine Tudor details, including panelling and furniture. *(May-Sep)*

Broughton Castle stands on an island site surrounded by a 3 acre moat.

3 Upton House

The main attraction of this house is the wonderful art collection and tapestries collected by the Viscount Bearsted. The terraced gardens, including a traditional kitchen garden, are also worth a stroll. *(Mar-Oct)*

4 Sulgrave Manor

In the 16th century Sulgrave Manor was home to a family that can count George Washington among its descendants. This connection is now the main focus of the house, and its small museum is devoted to Washington and American politics. *(Feb-Dec)*

Sulgrave Manor: the home of George Washington's Ancestors.

The circular temple at Stowe Gardens.

5 Stowe Gardens

Landscape gardening was a passion in the 18th century and Stowe is one of the finest examples – Alexander Pope was among the many who extolled its virtues. *(Mar-Oct)*

Local attractions/events:

Open all year (except some public holidays) unless otherwise shown

Banbury:

The Mill: North Oxfordshire's foremost entertainment venue for arts, theatre, music, dance, comedy and events

Surrounding areas:
(also refer to pages 117, 133 & 147)

Heritage Motor Centre, *North of Banbury:* a unique collection of over 200 classic and historic British cars, with themed exhibitions

National Herb Centre, *Warmington:* over 400 different varieties growing in fields, gardens and the plant centre, described in greater detail in the Exhibition *(Mar-Dec)*

Bloxham Village Museum: reflects aspects of past life, with a new exhibition every six months *(restricted days)*

Aynho Park, *Aynho:* a grand 17th century house, home of the Cartwright family, with a selection of ground floor rooms open to the public *(limited days, May-Sep)*

Rousham House, *nr Steeple Aston:* uncommercialised 17th century house and gardens, containing over 150 portraits and fine contemporary furniture *(limited days, Apr-Sep)*

Farnborough Hall, *Farnborough:* 18th century house and gardens, home of the Holbech family for over 300 years *(limited days, Apr-Sep)*

Bygones Museum, *Claydon:* displays of local rural life and bygone days, with regular 'steam' events in the summer

Silverstone: Formula One racing at its very best – the racetrack for the British Grand Prix

Bicester Village: with its purpose-built New England 'designer' outlet shopping centre

A Murder Mystery Weekend hotel – see pages 34-35

Heritage Hotels – Bath

The Bath Spa Hotel

Sydney Road, Bath, Somerset BA2 6JF *See map page 3*
Tel: (0)870 400 8222 Fax: (0)122 544 4006
Regional General Manager: Michael Grange E-mail: HeritageHotels_Bath.Bath_Spa@forte-hotels.com
Reservations: (0)870 400 8855 www.heritage-hotels.com

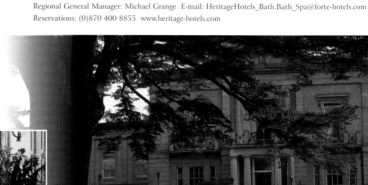

How to get there:

Exit the M4 at junction 18 onto the A46 following signs to Bath until the roundabout. Turn right onto the A4 following city centre signs. At the first major set of traffic lights, turn left towards the A36. At the mini-roundabout, turn right then next left after Holburne Museum into Sydney Place. The hotel is 200 yards up the hill on the right.

Facilities: 98 bedrooms, 6 four-posters, 7 suites, 24-hour room service, mini-bar, hairdryer, satellite TV, 2 Restaurants *(non-smoking)*, 2 bars, drawing room, Health and Leisure Spa with indoor heated pool, gymnasium and 3 beauty rooms, hairdressing salon, croquet lawn, tennis court, chauffeur and car valet service, free car park.
Family: Baby sitting, Nursery in hotel grounds for 2–7 yr olds.

Once an elegant private house dating back to the 1830s, this hotel is fronted by a long sweeping driveway and seven acres of landscaped gardens. A Mediterranean-style menu is served informally in the Alfresco Restaurant, amid murals and exotic plants, overlooking the gardens. The Vellore Restaurant, once a ballroom and host to the season's sparkling debutantes, offers traditional English fare in an elegant setting.

Leisure rates pppn

Midweek:	BB	DBB
Apr 2000	£ 75	£ 95
May–Jun	£ 85	£105
Jul–Aug	£ 75	£ 95
Sept–Nov	£ 85	£105
Dec–Mar 2001	£ 65	£ 85
Weekend:	BB	DBB
Apr–Jun 2000	£120	£140
Jul–Aug	£115	£135
Sept–Nov	£125	£145
Dec–Mar 2001	£105	£125

Pure Indulgence Break:

What's included in your break:
• 2 nights' accommodation
• dinner each evening in either the Alfresco or Vellore restaurants (wine not included)
• full traditional breakfast each morning
• a bottle of chilled champagne, a box of home-made chocolates and a bouquet of flowers in the room on arrival
• tickets for the open-topped bus tour of Bath

Pure Indulgence Break rates:

Validity dates:
all dates until 20 December 2000
Mid-week from £240 per person for two nights
Weekends from £320 per person for two nights
Upgrade to a suite or four-poster room, supplement of £150 for two nights
(rates apply to two people sharing and subject to availability)
Please quote 'Special Break' when booking.

Bath – Somerset

1 American Museum

A series of 18 furnished rooms provide an authentic insight into how Americans lived in the 17th-19th centuries. A purpose-built centre hosts a range of temporary exhibitions whilst outside in the beautiful gardens, based on George Washington's in Virginia, there are living re-enactments of civil war battles during the summer. *(Mar-Oct)*

2 Longleat House and Safari Park

The country home of the Marquess of Bath, this Elizabethan mansion is open to the public. Treasures include a vast private library and a collection of Old Masters. The surrounding woodland, landscaped by Lancelot 'Capability' Brown, has been converted into a safari park, including lions, tigers and elephants. House open all year. *(Park attractions, Apr-Oct only)*

3 Wells

Britain's smallest city is famed for its 13th century cathedral, decorated with more than 300 medieval sculptures.

Wells Cathedral.

4 Cheddar Caves & Gorge

Huge limestone cliffs reaching a height of 450ft soar above the road to the north of the town of Cheddar. The caves, gouged out by an underground river, are filled with stalactites and stalagmites.

5 Bristol

Bristol has thrived as a port since the 11th century. Today it is an elegant city of art galleries, museums, cafés and theatres. The Clifton Suspension Bridge, designed by the great engineer Isambard Kingdom Brunel, spans the River Avon.

Local attractions/events:
Open all year (except some public holidays) unless otherwise shown

Bath: *(also refer to page 57)*

Prior Park Gardens: enjoy an exhilarating walk through these landscaped gardens and the breathtaking views of Bath and the Avon Valley

Dyrham Park: built between 1692-1702, it is furnished in the Dutch style *(paintings and Delftware)* with new rooms on display for 2000

International Music Fair: 17 days of the world's best and most varied music in magnificent surroundings *(19th May-4th June)*

Jane Austen Centre: an insight into her life and aspirations

St George's Day Lunch: Bath Spa Hotel *(23rd May)*

A Toast to English Wine: Bath Spa Hotel *(1-31st May)*

Surrounding areas:

Stourhead Gardens & House: *nr Warminster:* world famous Palladian mansion with magnificent art and furniture collections

Wookey Hole Caves & Papermill, *nr Wells:* spectacular Showcaves, Victorian Papermill and Neptune's Kingdom are just some of the many attractions

Chewton Cheese Dairy, *Chewton Mendip:* see (and taste!) traditional Cheddar and other national cheeses in the making

Bradford on Avon: 14th century Tithe Barn, Medieval Bridge, Kennet and Avon Canal Museum and lots more

Stanton Drew Stone Circle: along with Stonehenge & Avebury, this represents one of the world's most mysterious wonders

Ilford Manor Gardens, *Westwood:* award winning gardens of genuine character. Tudor house on the banks of the River Frome *(Apr-Oct)*

Heritage Hotels – Bath

The Francis

Queen Square, Bath, Somerset BA1 2HH *See map page 3*
Tel: (0)870 400 8223 Fax: (0)122 531 9715
Regional General Manager: Michael Grange E-mail: HeritageHotels_Bath.Francis@forte-hotels.com
Reservations: (0)870 400 8855 www.heritage-hotels.com

How to get there:
The Francis is located in Queen Square, a short distance from the Circus. Simply follow the A4 through route, which forms the north side of Queen Square.

Facilities: 94 bedrooms, 1 suite, 2 mini-suites, Square restaurant, Caffebar and Lounge, free car park *(limited spaces).*
Family: Baby sitting by prior arrangement

Leisure rates pppn

Midweek:	BB	DBB
Apr 2000	£ 59	£ 79
May–Aug	£ 64	£ 84
Sep–Nov	£ 59	£ 79
Dec–Feb	£ 54	£ 74
March 2001	£ 59	£ 79
Weekend:	**BB**	**DBB**
Apr 2000	£ 64	£ 84
May–Aug	£ 69	£ 89
Sep–Nov	£ 64	£ 84
Dec–Feb	£ 59	£ 79
March 2001	£ 64	£ 84

Curtain Call Break rates

Supplement of £25 per person on the Leisure Break rates
Validity dates:
Subject to availability of theatre performances
Please quote 'Special Break' when booking.

The Francis is the epitome of Georgian elegance in the very heart of the city of Bath. Located in Queen Square, the hotel offers you the enviable position of being within walking distance of Bath's major attractions. These include weekly antiques fairs, Bath Abbey, Costume Museum, The Royal Crescent and fine shopping.

Curtain Call at the Francis on the Square Break:

Combine your stay at the Francis with an evening of entertainment at the Theatre Royal, widely recognised as one of the finest provincial theatres in the country. The theatre boasts a varied programme of one-week runs, many of which are pre- or post- the West End of London. Whether you are an avid theatre-goer or an occasional enthusiast, you are sure to find plenty to choose from, and for a theatre break in Bath, you cannot get closer than the Francis.

Curtain Call includes one top-price ticket for the Theatre Royal, including a glass of champagne on your return to the Francis.

Bath – Somerset

1 Royal Crescent

This elegant semi-circle of houses was the first crescent to be built in Britain. Thirty houses are lined with Ionic columns along their façades. Number 1 Royal Crescent has been carefully restored to reflect its original Georgian glory.

2 The Assembly Rooms

This fine building is home to a fascinating Museum of Costume, ranging from 16th century clothing to modern-day fashions.

3 Roman Baths and Pump Room

Britain's only hot spring was turned into a sacred site by the Romans, around which they built these baths and a temple to serve pilgrims and the sick. They are now the finest Roman remains in Britain. The adjacent Pump Room was a popular 18th century meeting place for Bath's fashionable society, and is now a tearoom.

Any first-time trip to Bath is not complete without a visit to the impressive Roman Baths.

4 Bath Abbey

The 16th century Bath Abbey, built on the site of a former Norman church, is typical of the Gothic Perpendicular architectural style, complete with fan vaulting. The abbey's tower reaches a height of 162ft.

5 Pulteney Bridge

No visitor to Bath can miss the importance of the River Avon to the city, with its beautiful Italianate bridge crossing the weir.

Bath's beautiful Italianate Pulteney Bridge crossing the weir at night.

Local attractions/events:

Open all year (except some public holidays) unless otherwise shown

Bath: *(also refer to page 55)*

Holburne Museum of Art: historic building housing 17th and 18th century fine art and Old Master paintings

Racecourse: numerous meetings between May and October

Mumfords Vineyard: a delightful setting overlooking the Avon Valley – where better to sample the grape?

Walcot & Broad Streets: this is the area to shop if you seek a variety of unusual arts, crafts, bric-a-brac or antiques

Upper Town: many specialist fairs feature here during the year, including Decorative Antiques *(March)* and the Book Fair *(October)*

Farmers' Market: locally grown produce available every 1st and 3rd Saturday, held in Green Park Station

A Taste of the West Country: Francis Hotel *(19th-26th May)*

Herb Market and the Taste of Summer: Francis Hotel *(1-30th June)*

Surrounding areas:

(also refer to pages 67 & 127)

Glastonbury Tor & Abbey: thought to be the burial place of King Arthur and Queen Guinevere, it is now more 'legendary' as an annual rock festival venue *(June)*

Haynes Motor Museum, *Sparkford:* over 250 exhibits, it is Britain's most spectacular collection of Automobilia

Fleet Air Arm Museum, *Yeovil:* one of the world's greatest aviation museums, with a highly imaginative collection of exhibits and stories

Radstock Museum, *Radstock:* exhibition of the local social, mining and family heritage

Lacock Abbey & Museum: 17th century abbey converted into a fine country house and the Fox Talbot Museum of Photography

A Murder Mystery Weekend hotel – see pages 34-37

(Map of Bath showing: Royal Crescent, Upper Church Street, Circus Mews, Russel St, Assembly Rooms, Brock Street, The Circus, Bennett Street, Lansdown Rd, Saville Row, No 1 Royal Crescent (Museum), Alfred St, Hay Hill, Bartlett St, Paragon, Gay Street, George St, Broad St, Queen's Parade Place, Old King Street, National Centre of Photography, Grove St, Charlotte Street, Queen Square, Wood St, Quiet St, Green St, Pulteney Bridge, Argyle St, Puppet Theatre, Chapel Row, Barton Street, New Bond St, Upper Borough Walls, Bridge St, Grand Parade, Avon, Weir, Princes St, The Francis, Union Pas, Union St, Cheap St, Westgate Street, Stall St, Guildhall, Art Gallery & Market, Abbey, Bath St, Roman Baths & Pump Room)

Heritage Hotels – Box Hill

The Burford Bridge

The Foot of Box Hill, Dorking, Surrey RH5 6BX *See map page 4*
Tel: (0)870 400 8283 Fax: (0)130 688 0386 Regional General Manager: Caroline Bellenger
E-mail: HeritageHotels_Box_Hill.Burford_Bridge@forte-hotels.com
Reservations: (0)870 400 8855 www.heritage-hotels.com

How to get there:
Four miles from junction 9 off the M25 on the A24 at the foot of Box Hill.

Facilities: 57 bedrooms, 24-hour room service, hairdryer, trouser press, restaurant, bar, lounge, open fires in winter, heated outdoor pool *(May–September)*, Tithe Barn with minstrel's gallery available for special events, free car park.
Family: Baby listening, baby sitting.

Every mellow brick of this ancient gem glows with history. It was here that Lord Nelson spent secret hours with his great love Emma Hamilton before going off to his last battle at Trafalgar. It nestles at the foot of a famous beauty spot, Box Hill, with Mole River running at the bottom of its spectacular gardens. Spot the clues about fellow guests in intriguing Murder Mystery Weekends. Rail service to London takes 40 minutes.

Wine Tasting Break:

Arrive at the Burford Bridge at your leisure in the afternoon. Check in to your room and enjoy a cream tea in the fabulous lounge, or, weather permitting, in the lovely gardens, and a swim in the pool.

A 3-course dinner awaits you in the one-rosette restaurant – the Emlyn Room.

Following breakfast, make your way to Denbie Wine Estate and enjoy a tour and wine tasting at this award-winning vineyard.

Then, why not take a walk up Box Hill at your leisure?

After such an enjoyable day, the Emlyn Room Restaurant is again the setting for your evening dinner. After a good night's sleep, breakfast is served before your departure. On your way home, stop at Polesden Lacey to see this historic house.

What's included in your break:
• 2 nights' dinner, bed and breakfast
• champagne and flowers in your room on arrival
• 3-course dinner in the restaurant each night
• full English breakfast both days
• entry and wine tasting at Denbies Wine Estate
• entry to Polesden Lacey
• afternoon tea on arrival
• swimming pool – free entrance – 1 May–30 September, weather permitting

Leisure rates pppn

	BB	DBB
Midweek:		
Apr–Mar 2001	£165	£185
Weekend:	BB	DBB
Apr–Mar 2001	£ 55	£ 65

Special Break rates

Weekends only, plus any 2 nights 19 July–28 August 2000 £160 per person for two nights (based on two people sharing)
Please quote 'Special Break' when booking.

58

Box Hill – Surrey

1 Box Hill

This tall mound in the heart of Surrey has always been a popular day-trip location, not least for its fine views across the county. In winter, both children and adults can be seen 'sledging' down the slopes whenever the hill is covered with snow.

2 Denbies Wine Estate

Like a good wine, there is more to Denbies than meets the eye. Nestling in the beautiful Mole Valley, it is England's largest vineyard, producing over 400,000 bottles a year. Experience the incredible audio-visual presentation, a guided tour by train and, naturally, sample the goods!

The Atrium Restaurant is very popular with visitors to Denbies Wine Estate.

3 Polesden Lacey

This Regency house, built in the 1820s, was the home of the society hostess, Mrs Ronnie Greville at the turn of the 20th century. Visited by royalty and the rich and famous, Polesden Lacey was the site of high society partying. *(Mar-Oct)*

4 Clandon Park

This Palladian villa, inspired by the Italian architect Andrea Palladio, was built in the 18th century for the Onslow family. Inside the house is a fine collection of English porcelain. The impressive grounds around the house include a Maori meeting house, which the Earl of Onslow brought back with him from New Zealand in the 19th century. *(Mar-Oct)*

The house at Clandon Park seen from the south west.

The red brick, west front of the house at Hatchlands Park.

5 Hatchlands Park

Built in 1758, the house contains splendid interiors by Robert Adam, appropriately decorated in a naval style. It boasts the Cobbe Collection – the world's largest group of keyboard instruments, associated with such names as Bach, Chopin, Purcell, Mahler and Elgar. *(Apr-Oct)*

Local attractions/events:

Open all year (except some public holidays) unless otherwise shown

Surrounding areas:

(also refer to pages 75 & 97)

Museum of Local History,
Leatherhead: located in a 17th century timber-framed house *(Apr-Dec)*

Fire & Iron Gallery,
Leatherhead: watch blacksmiths ply their art, especially in the design of jewellery items

Thorndike Theatre,
Leatherhead: productions include all-star casts prior to London's West End transfer

Semaphore Tower,
Chatley Heath: unique Naval Telegraph Station, includes guided tours and demonstrations *(Mar-Oct)*

Chessington World of Adventure: one of the country's leading theme parks – an exciting day out for all the family *(Apr-Oct)*

Epsom Racecourse: the 'Derby' is a highlight of the equestrian calendar, run on the first Saturday in June *(Mar-Oct)*

The Derby Experience: Epsom trainers agree to behind-the-scene tours for about 20 days of the year

Epsom Downs: race days apart, this venue also hosts a variety of events throughout the year – craft, toy and antiques fairs and even live music festivals!

Bourne Hall Museum,
Ewell: set in rambling gardens, it covers two millenia of local history

The Queen's Royal Surrey Regiment Museum,
Clandon Park: housed in this National Trust property, it documents the story of the infantry regiments of Surrey over the centuries *(Mar-Oct)*

A Murder Mystery Weekend hotel – see pages 34-37

Hennessy
X.O
The masterpiece
of achievement

Heritage Hotels – Camberley

Frimley Hall

Lime Ave, off Portsmouth Road, Camberley, Surrey GU15 2BG *See map page 4*
Tel: (0)870 400 8224 Fax: (0)127 669 1253 General Manager: Adam Terpening
E-mail: HeritageHotels_Camberley.Frimley_Hall@forte-hotels.com
Reservations: (0)870 400 8855 www.heritage-hotels.com

How to get there:
Leave the M3 at junction 3 and follow the A30 west to the Mongolian Barbecue. Branch left onto the A325 and then turn right into Conifer Drive and Lime Avenue to the Frimley Hall Hotel.

Facilities: 86 bedrooms, 1 four-poster, 1 half-tester, 3 half-canopies, 15 family bedrooms, hairdryer, trouser press, Wellington Restaurant, bar, free car park.
Local leisure facilities: indoor swimming pool, squash, gym, snooker, table tennis, horse-riding and golf.
Family: Baby listening.

This is a classic ivy-clad Victorian manor set in four acres of beautiful gardens with green velvety lawns. Its timeless air and gracious setting are just half an hour from Heathrow Airport and are guaranteed to have a calming effect on the ragged nerves of any jet-lagged business executives. For those getting married, you can now have both the wedding ceremony and the reception at Frimley Hall. Or simply settle for a drink in the Sandhurst Bar and a fine traditional meal in the Wellington Restaurant. A grand, ornately carved staircase leads to rooms with leaded windows and inlaid mahogany furniture.

Leisure rates pppn

Midweek:	BB	DBB
Apr–Mar 2001	£ 99	£116
Weekend:	BB	DBB
Apr–Mar 2001	£ 45	£ 55

Special Break rates

Weekends only, plus any 2 nights 21 July–28 August 2000 £150 per person for two nights *(based on two people sharing)* **Please quote 'Special Break' when booking.**

Gardens Break:

Arrive at Frimley Hall at your leisure in the afternoon. Check in to your room and enjoy a cream tea in the fabulous lounge. A 3-course dinner awaits you in the Wellington Restaurant.
Following breakfast, make your way to Wisley Gardens and enjoy a gentle, or not so gentle, walk around the extensive grounds owned by the Royal Horticultural Society.
After such an enjoyable day, the Wellington Restaurant is again the setting for your evening dinner. After a good night's sleep, breakfast is served before your departure. On your way home, stop at Birdworld at Farnham to see the many exotic birds and the many other attractions at this venue.

What's included in your break:
• 2 nights' dinner, bed and breakfast
• champagne and flowers in your room on arrival
• 3-course dinner in the restaurant each night
• full English breakfast both days
• entry to Wisley Gardens
• entry to Birdworld
• afternoon tea on arrival

Camberley – Surrey

1 Sandhurst

This small town is best known for the Royal Military Academy. Its harsh regime to produce the finest and the best soldiers is part of English lore. The Academy Museum, which includes exhibits of uniforms and medals of Imperial armies, is particularly popular with children.

3 Loseley Hall

The 16th century home of the More family abounds with original Tudor details such as panelling, plaster ceilings and a Great Hall. Elizabeth I and James I both stayed here. It also features many fine works of art and the restored walled garden contains roses, herbs, flowers, fountains and a moat walk. *(May-Aug)*

Surrounding areas:
(also refer to pages 51 & 85)

Local attractions/events:

Open all year (except some public holidays) unless otherwise shown

Surrey Heath Museum, *Camberley:* a small but attractively designed museum, through a number of permanent displays, it depicts local history and the environment

Basingstoke Canal Visitor Centre, *Mychett:* family attractions, exhibitions and special events calendar, together with canal cruises *(by narrow boat)*

Army Medical Services Museum, *Ash Vale:* possibly not for the faint-hearted, it traces the history of army medicine and associated treatments from 1660, with exhibits

Guildford Discovery: friendly hands-on science centre where you can have great fun interacting with the exhibits

Guildford Museum: step into the world of prehistoric man, the Romans, Saxons, Victorians and, more surprisingly, Lewis Caroll

Finchampstead Ridges, *Crowthorne:* a popular venue for walkers, offering impressive views across the Thames basin

Hog's Back Brewery, *Tongham:* a traditional brewery since 1768 – take a tour, savour the atmosphere and sample the goods

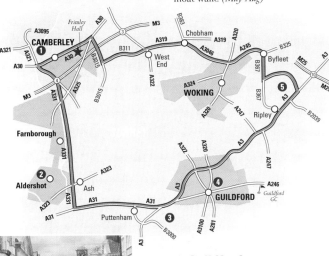

The famous overhanging clock in Guildford High Street.

2 Aldershot Military Museum

This museum exhibits details of military life in the area since 1854. Army transport from horses to World War II armoured carriers are also on display. Nearby Farnborough is the site of the bi-annual airshow, a highlight for anyone with an interest in aerospace.

4 Guildford

This ancient town and its environs is well worth a lengthy visit in its own right. It retains much of its historic charm, with cobbled streets and the remnants of a once imposing hill castle and also offers a cosmopolitan flavour of restaurants, bars, cafés and extensive shopping facilities.

5 Wisley Gardens

These beautiful gardens were created in 1878 as an experiment in growing "difficult" plants. Collections of plants from around the world still thrive in this unlikely spot, including rock gardens, alpine gardens and Japanese gardens, as well as modern-style gardens.

Rhododendron bushes in full flower at Wisley Gardens.

A Murder Mystery Weekend hotel – see pages 34-37

Heritage Hotels – Canterbury

The Chaucer Hotel

Ivy Lane, Canterbury, Kent CT1 1TU *See map page 5*
Tel: (0)870 400 8106 Fax: (0)122 745 0397
General Manger: David Thompson E-mail: HeritageHotels_Canterbury.Chaucer_Hotel@forte-hotels.com
Reservations: (0)870 400 8855 www.heritage-hotels.com

How to get there:

Canterbury is situated 10 miles from the end of the M2. The Chaucer is in Ivy Lane, on the left of Lower Chantry Lane, on the eastern side of the city wall.

Facilities: 42 bedrooms, hairdryer, trouser press, restaurant, bar/lounge, free car park.
Family: Baby listening, baby sitting.

Leisure rates pppn

Midweek:	BB	DBB
Apr 2000	£ 60	£ 75
May–Jun	£ 60	£ 70
Jul–Nov	£ 65	£ 75
Dec–Feb	£ 55	£ 65
March 2001	£ 60	£ 70
Weekend:	BB	DBB
Apr–Jun 2000	£ 55	£ 70
Jul–Aug	£ 65	£ 80
Sept–Nov	£ 55	£ 70
Dec–Feb	£ 55	£ 65
March 2001	£ 55	£ 70

Special Break validity dates

Weekends only from June 200–end March 2001
Please quote 'Special Break' when booking.

Originally The Chaucer was a private Georgian house standing opposite Canterbury's ancient city walls. All the en-suite bedrooms in this historic hotel are named after Chaucer's characters. Canterbury is deeply woven into the fabric of English history and even before medieval times it had always attracted religious pilgrims, a tradition particularly relevant in this Millennium year. Visit Canterbury Cathedral or take a punt trip on the river. Good shopping.

Canterbury Tales Break:

Stay two nights at the weekend on the leisure break rate and you'll receive two free tickets to enjoy the Canterbury Tales, one of Britain's most popular attractions.

A visit to Canterbury Tales is just like returning to medieval England, with its stunning reconstructions of 14th-century Canterbury. Inside this historic building you can step back into medieval Canterbury with all its splendours.

Here you can join Geoffrey Chaucer (the hotel's namesake and England's finest poet) and his colourful characters as they journey towards the shrine of St Thomas Becket and Canterbury Cathedral.

Canterbury – Kent

1 **Canterbury Cathedral**

The headquarters of the Church of England, Canterbury Cathedral was begun in 1070 and still dominates the city. The shrine of St Thomas à Becket commemorates the assassinated saint who formed the subject for T.S. Eliot's *Murder in the Cathedral*. There are abundant decorative features from the 14th to the 16th centuries.

3 **Sissinghurst Castle Garden**

The grounds of this Elizabethan manor were lovingly landscaped into one of England's finest gardens. Separate areas have different "themes", such as the "White Garden", with white and silver flowers.

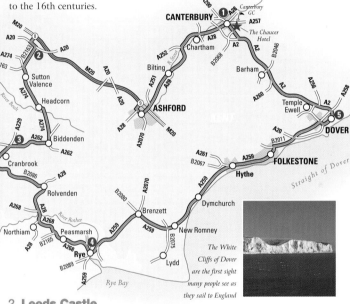

The White Cliffs of Dover are the first sight many people see as they sail to England

2 **Leeds Castle**

This Norman fortress is best known for its magnificent setting, half on an island in the middle of a lake and surrounded by gardens and a traditional English maze. Once a royal property, the castle is now used for social functions.

Leeds castle in autumn.

4 **Rye**

One of the most picturesque towns in England achieves most of its charm from its hilly layout and cobbled streets. Tudor buildings, medieval churches and a small castle all add to the atmosphere.

5 **Dover**

First established as a town by the Romans, the main attraction is its 12th century castle complex. From the top of the Keep there are views across the Channel to France. The 'White Cliffs Experience' will give you a greater insight into the area.

Local attractions/events:
Open all year (except some public holidays) unless otherwise shown

Canterbury:

Heritage Museum: an enthralling time-walk linking great events, famous people and precious objects from the city's 2000 year history
Roman Museum: innovative underground exhibition, which includes reconstructions of Roman buildings, mosaics and artefacts
Canterbury Tales Visitor Attraction: step back into the 14th century; experience the sounds and smells of medieval England
The Chaucer Centre: set in a 15th century building, visitors are encouraged to discover the world of this famous author's 'Canterbury Tales' through exploration of his work, life and times

Surrounding areas:

Elham Valley Vineyard, *Barham:* jams, mustards, pottery and handicrafts are some of the items available – and wine, of course!
Howletts Wild Animal Parks, *nr Hythe:* includes the largest captive gorilla breeding group
Lamb House, *Rye:* literary haven of the Anglo-American writer Henry James *(Mar-Oct)*
Scotney Castle Garden, *Lamberhurst:* 14th century moated castle ruin set in extensive parkland, meadows, woods and hopfields *(Mar-Oct)*
Kent Battle of Britain Museum, *nr Folkestone:* the largest collection of exhibits and artefacts in the country *(Apr-Nov)*
Folkestone Racecourse: year round racing for lovers of the sport
Walmer Castle and Gardens: an elegant Tudor residence, still used by HM Queen Mother *(Apr-Oct)*

A Music at Leisure Weekend hotel – see pages 32-33
A Murder Mystery Weekend hotel – see pages 34-37

Heritage Hotels – Cheltenham

The Queen's

The Promenade, Cheltenham, Gloucestershire GL50 1NN *See map page 7*
Tel: (0)870 400 8107 Fax: (0)1242 224 145 General Manager: Stephanie Hocking
E-mail: HeritageHotels_Cheltenham.Queens@forte-hotels.com
Reservations: (0)870 400 8855 www.heritage-hotels.com

How to get there:
The Queen's is close to the town centre, just opposite the Ladies' College and at the junction of the Promenade and Imperial Square.

Facilities: 73 rooms, 2 four-poster rooms, 4 executive feature rooms, 24-hour room service, hairdryer, trouser press, satellite TV, Napier Restaurant, Le Petit Blanc Restaurant, bar, lounge, garden views, free car park *(for residents)*. Guests on dinner-inclusive rates dine in the Napier Restaurant.

Family: Baby listening, baby sitting.

Leisure rates pppn

Midweek:	BB	DBB
Apr–Jun 2000	£ 70	£ 75
Jul–Aug	£ 60	£ 65
Sep–Nov	£ 70	£ 75
Dec–Feb	£ 60	£ 65
March 2001	£ 70	£ 75
Weekend:	BB	DBB
Apr–Jun 2000	£ 55	£ 70
Jul–Aug	£ 50	£ 65
Sep–Nov	£ 55	£ 70
Dec–Feb	£ 50	£ 65
March 2001	£ 55	£ 70

Petit Blanc rates
Add £10 to DBB rates to dine at Le Petit Blanc.

Wine and Water Break rates
£175 per person for two nights
Bonus Night *(Sunday)*:
£45 per person

This elegant hotel commands a spectacular position at the top of the tree-lined promenade of Cheltenham Spa. The town itself is the most complete Regency Town in Britain, with over 2000 listed buildings, and is the gateway to the picturesque Cotswolds. The Queen's is renowned as a venue for traditional afternoon teas in the lounge, and top chef Raymond Blanc's Le Petit Blanc brasserie provides an exciting and informal alternative to the more serene setting of the hotel's Napier Restaurant.

Wine and Water Break:

A weekend with a difference - the fascinating world of wine-making plus historical British waterways.

Day 1 – A short car journey to Newent takes you to the Three Choirs Vineyard in the glorious Gloucestershire countryside. Your visit includes a tour of the vineyard with a video presentation and tasting followed by a delicious lunch in the Vineyard Restaurant, which has been awarded two AA rosettes.

Day 2 – Visit Gloucester Docks, the most inland port in Britain. The docks have now been subject to a gentle and thoughtful restoration programme, which has included the development of the National Waterways Museum. This award-winning museum tells the 200-year story of the inland waterways through lively displays and interactive exhibits.

You will enjoy exploring the five-floored antiques centre and entry has also been arranged into the Robert Opie Collection, a nostalgic look at advertising and packaging, where you can see the packs, bottles and tins of your childhood. What's included in your break:

• accommodation in a twin or double room on Friday and Saturday
• 3-course dinner each evening
• full English breakfast each morning
• tour, tasting and Saturday lunch at Three Choirs
• entrance to the National Waterways Museum and the Robert Opie Collection
• a mixed case of a dozen Three Choirs wines delivered direct to your home on your return

Please quote 'Special Break' when booking.

Cheltenham – Gloucestershire

1 Cheltenham

In the 19th century, Cheltenham was one of the most popular and elegant towns in England, high society being attracted by its restorative spa water. Today the town is probably best known for its racecourse, which buzzes in March during its National Hunt Festival.

2 Gloucester

Gloucester Cathedral was built in 1327 and is probably best known as the burial site of the murdered king, Edward II. Gloucester Docks area was originally created as a corn-trading centre in the 19th century, during the Industrial Revolution.

The old warehouses have now been carefully restored and converted into museums, shops and restaurants.

3 Stroud

England's cloth, wool and textile industries were all largely centred around Stroud, and many of its former mills are still standing – some now converted to luxury loft-style accommodations. A museum in the town details the industrial history.

4 Cirencester

This ancient Roman city revolves around its Market Place, which made it a thriving centre of trade. A 15th century church and several 17th and 18th century houses make it an attractive place to visit.

The 14th century Gloucester Cathedral was the final resting place for the murdered King Edward II.

5 Sudeley Castle

Sudeley Castle has strong connections with the monarchy – Charles I found refuge here during the Civil War and, some years earlier, the last of Henry VIII's six wives, the widowed Catherine Parr, lived here as the wife of Lord Sudeley. Artefacts within the house document its rich past.

Local attractions/events:
Open all year (except some public holidays) unless otherwise shown

Cheltenham:

Art Gallery and Museum: world-renowned Arts and Crafts Movement collection, including furniture and metal work, local archaeological treasures and town history

Pittville Pump Room and Park: This magnificent building, completed in 1830, offers visitors the opportunity to sample both the town's famous spa waters – or live music

Holst Birthplace Museum: details the life of the composer of 'The Planets'

Racecourse: home of National Hunt Racing *(Oct–Apr)* although meetings take place all year

Festival of Literature: this annual event in October includes lectures, poetry readings, workshops, films, exhibitions and literary tours

Surrounding areas:
(also refer to pages 133 & 147)

The Cotswolds: a cornucopia of picturesque towns and villages, notably Bibury, Northleach, The Slaughters, Stow-on-the-Wold, Moreton-in-Marsh, Chipping Campden, Broadway and Stanton

Rococo Garden Trust, *Painswick:* unique 18th century garden with an abundant array of gardens and woodland *(Jan–Nov)*

Hailes Abbey, *Winchcombe:* this Cistercian abbey was built in the 13th century and subsequently demolished until excavated in the 19th century – now a fascinating museum waiting to be discovered

Corinium Museum, *Cirencester:* one of the finest collections of antiquities from Roman Britain. Includes reconstructions, displays and exhibitions

A Music at Leisure Weekend hotel – see pages 32-33

67

Heritage Hotels – Chester

Blossoms Hotel

St John's Street, Chester, Cheshire CH1 1HL *See map page 7*
Tel: (0)870 400 8108 Fax: (0)124 434 6433 Regional General Manager: Debbie Johnson
E-mail: HeritageHotels_Chester.Blossoms@forte-hotels.com
Reservations: (0)870 400 8855 www.heritage-hotels.com

How to get there:
From junction 12 of the M53 follow signs for the city centre. St John's Street is off Eastgate Street (which is signposted from the ring road) at the centre of the shopping and pedestrianised area.

Facilities: 64 bedrooms, 1 suite, 1 four-poster, 1 half-tester, room service, hairdryer, restaurant, bar, lounge, NCP car park nearby *(special free 24-hour pass provided by hotel).*
Family: Baby listening, baby sitting.

Blossoms lies at the very heart of the medieval walled city of Chester. Its popularity dates back to the last century, when Chester became an area for fashionable folk who demanded elegant, spacious accommodation. The same atmosphere remains here, amid high ceilings, a sweeping staircase, potted plants, and the scene-setting music from the pianist in the Brookes Restaurant. A walk along the city walls is not to be missed. Visit the sandy beaches of the North Wales coastline.

Leisure rates pppn

Midweek:	BB	DBB
Apr 2000	£ 50	£ 65
May–Nov	£ 55	£ 70
Dec–Feb	£ 45	£ 60
March 2001	£ 50	£ 65
Weekend:	BB	DBB
Apr 2000	£ 47	£ 62
May–Nov	£ 52	£ 67
Dec–Feb	£ 42	£ 57
March 2001	£ 47	£ 62

Special Break rates
Price per person, £150 for two nights
Please quote 'Special Break' when booking.

Special Break:
Blossoms was once the terminus of the London to Chester coach *("Stand and deliver!")*. Chester dates back to Roman times and the ancient sandstone Cathedral is worth a visit, while a walk along the walls is an experience not to be missed.

Enjoy a 3-course evening meal in either the stylish Brookes Restaurant or in the new Mongolian Barbecue Restaurant.

After a leisurely breakfast the next day, take a walk on the wild side! Visit the largest zoo in the country, home to many rare animals, open every day except Christmas day. A fun day out for everyone.

Return to the hotel for your evening meal. On the second day of your stay, after enjoying your breakfast, why not take an open-top bus tour of the city? A truly unique way to enjoy this historic city.

What's included in your break:
• 2 nights' dinner, bed and breakfast
• tickets for the open-top bus tour of the city
• tickets to the zoo for 2 adults and up to 2 children
• free accommodation for children sharing adults' room
• free meals for all children under the age of 5

Chester – Cheshire

1 Chester

The Tudor timbered buildings are the overriding image of this attractive northern town. Its history goes back further, to Roman times – and part of an old amphitheatre from this era can also be seen.

Eastgate clock in Chester.

2 Ellesmere Port

The prosperity of Chester stemmed from its access to canal and sea routes, making trading possible. The boat museum at Ellesmere Port details the history of canals and has a large number of historic barges on display.

3 Port Sunlight

Situated in the Wirral penninsula, Port Sunlight is one of the many timeless and picturesque garden villages that can be found in typical English countryside. It was founded by the soap manufacturer Lord Leverhulme for his factory workers.

4 Knutsford

Dating back to the Vikings, Knutsford is now best known as the home of the 19th century novelist Elizabeth Gaskell. She used the town as the basis of her novel *Cranford*. Close to Knutsford is the Jodrell Bank Observatory housing one of the world's largest radio telescopes; it tracks spacecraft and satellites and studies the radio universe.

5 Salford

The early 20th century artist Lowry encapsulated the industrial landscape of Manchester in his highly individual works of 'matchstick' workers. His home town is now given over to a fine art gallery, which exhibits some of his best paintings.

The houses of Port Sunlight are renowned for their architectural detail.

Local attractions/events:

Open all year (except some public holidays) unless otherwise shown

Chester:

Cathedral: exhibitions and audio visual presentation of Gothic architectural styles dating back to 1092
Visitor & Craft Centre: a great insight into local history/crafts with the help of a video presentation
Dewa Roman Experience: step aboard a Roman Galley or stroll along a reconstructed street and experience the sights, sounds and smells of the time
Toy & Doll Museum: a treasure-house of antique playthings
Grosvenor Museum: explore the city's past at this award-winning venue (re-opens summer 2000)
Zoo: new attractions for 2000
Racecourse: Britain's oldest racecourse *(Apr-Sep)*

Surrounding areas:

Erdigg Hall, *nr Wrexham:* depicts country house lifestyle in its heyday
Chirk Castle, *nr Wrexham:* a 14th century fortress with awe-inspiring staterooms and dungeons
Stapeley Water Gardens, *Nantwich:* three attractions in one – Europe's largest water gardens
Cheshire Farm Ice Cream Dairy, *Tattenhall:* a tasty change from the more famous local cheese
Quarry Bank Mill, *Styal:* authentic recreation of the workings of a Georgian cotton mill
Granada Studios, *Manchester:* popular with fans of 'Coronation Street' where you can see the set and take part in the action
Beatlemania, *Liverpool:* the 'fab-four' memories continue to live on, especially with the annual Festival in August
Jodrell Bank, *nr Knutsford:* a Science Centre with fascinating displays and exhibitions and the 76m Lovell radio telescope
Ness Botanic Gardens, *Neston:* outstanding botanical gardens boasting seasonal flowers, shrubs and trees

Heritage Hotels – Coventry

Brandon Hall

Brandon, Warwickshire CV8 3FW *See map page 8*
Tel: (0)870 400 8105 Fax: (0)24 7654 4909 General Manager: Daniel Draisey
E-mail: HeritageHotels_Coventry.Brandon-Hall@forte-hotels.com
Reservations: (0)870 400 8855 www.heritage-hotels.com

How to get there:

Brandon sits on the A428, reachable via the A46 from the North or A45 from the South. Once on either the A45 or A46 follow the signs for Binley Woods into Brandon. At the foot of the hill, fork to the right past a garage; the hotel is 300 yards along on the right.

Facilities: 57 bedrooms,

1 four-poster, 2 executive feature rooms, 1 mini-suite, restaurant, bar, lounge, 6-court squash club, open fire in winter, mini-golf and croquet *(summer only)*, clay pigeon shooting and archery *(available on request and subject to minimum group size)*, free car park.

Family: Baby listening, baby

sitting by prior arrangement.

Leisure rates pppn

Midweek:	BB	DBB
Apr–Jun 2000	£ 60	£ 80
Jul–Aug	£ 50	£ 70
Sep–Feb	£ 60	£ 80
March 2001	£ 65	£ 80
Weekend:	BB	DBB
Apr–Jun 2000	£ 38	£ 55
Jul–Aug	£ 35	£ 52
Sep–Feb	£ 38	£ 55
March 2001	£ 40	£ 57

Britain's Motoring Heritage Break rates

£135 per person for two nights. Bonus night £28.50 per person *Please quote 'Special Break' when booking.*

An impressive tree-lined avenue forms the driveway to this 17th-century hotel set in 17 acres of woodland, once a shooting lodge belonging to Brandon Manor. The historic village is mentioned in the Domesday Book, and the Lodge's own sporting traditions continue with facilities for clay pigeon shooting, archery and croquet on the lawn.

The hotel is convenient for the NEC and Birmingham city centre and the NIA as well as Shakespeare's Stratford.

Britain's Motoring Heritage Break:

Come and explore the rich history of the motor industry in the Midlands while enjoying the wonderful food and relaxing atmosphere of Brandon Hall.

Day 1 – Visit the fascinating Coventry Motor Museum with its large collection of vehicles depicting the history of the city's motoring heritage. Step back in time with the fine collection of Vintage cars including Queen Mary's Daimler and come right up to date with the amazing Thrust II. A delicious picnic hamper with complimentary car kit is provided so that after your visit you can drive out into some of Warwickshire's beautiful countryside for your lunch.

Day 2 – After a hearty breakfast you have a choice

of two visits. Motorcycling enthusiasts can visit the National Motorcycle Museum between Coventry and Birmingham and admire some of the bikes that once led the world in engineering design. Alternatively there is the largest collection of historic British cars in the UK at The Heritage Motor Centre at Gaydon.

What's included in your break:

- accommodation in a twin or double room on Friday and Saturday night, 3-course dinner each evening and full English breakfast each morning
- entrance to Coventry Motor Museum and either the Heritage Motor Centre or the National Motorcycle Museum
- complimentary car rug or picnic hamper

Coventry – Warwickshire

1 Coventry Cathedral

During World War II, Coventry suffered more than any other city in England, and was virtually flattened by bombs from the Luftwaffe in 1940. In 1962 Sir Basil Spence built a new cathedral on the old site, which is considered one of the finest postwar buildings in the country. Modern stained glass and religious art add to the spectacle.

Old St Michael's Cathedral at Coventry.

2 Soho House

Home of the industrial pioneer Mathew Boulton, it has been carefully restored to its 18th century character and appearance. It also presents the chance to see Boulton's own products made in his nearby factory – ormulu clocks, vases, Sheffield plate and tableware. The meeting place of the most important scientists and engineers of the time (the Lunar Society), various displays inform us of his interests such as the steam engine he developed with James Watt.

3 Bosworth Battlefield

In 1485, Bosworth was the historic site of the battle between Richard III and the eventual victor, the future Henry VII. Today a visitors' centre recounts the life and times of these warring monarchs and details of their battle.

4 Leicester

A thriving Roman settlement in turn led to an important medieval town and the homes of the influential Earls of Leicester. Today the city is known for its large Asian community, who enhance the city with spicy aromas from the many curry houses and, during their Festival of Light (Diwali) in October, with fairy lights along the streets.

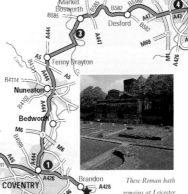

These Roman bath remains at Leicester are evidence of a once-thriving Roman settlement.

5 Melton Mowbray

The quintessentially English snack, the pork pie (minced pork covered in aspic and pastry) was created by the huntsmen of Melton Mowbray. Despite changing opinions on fox-hunting, pies are still made here and enjoyed around the country.

Local attractions/events:

Open all year (except some public holidays) unless otherwise shown

Coventry:

Lunt Roman Fort: Caelius the Soldier will guide you round this hill-top fort and tell you about his life nearly 2000 years ago

Museum of British Road Transport: the largest display of British made vehicles in the world, with over 500 exhibits

Canal Trail: a unique waterway experience, combining the natural peace of the countryside with the city's rich industrial heritage

Surrounding areas:

(also refer to pages 53 & 133)

Woombe Park, Binley: 400 acres of historic parkland which includes guided walks, lectures and an interactive discovery display

Jewellery Quarter, Birmingham: discover what life was like when the city was known as 'the workshop of the world'

Bourneville, nr Birmingham: the Cadbury family set up their famous chocolate-making factory here, and today the museum tour takes visitors through the production process – with a free tasting at the end!

A Music at Leisure Weekend
hotel – see pages 32-33
A Murder Mystery Weekend
hotel – see pages 34-37

Heritage Hotels – Dartmouth

The Dart Marina

Sandquay, Dartmouth, Devon TQ6 9PH *See map page 3*
Tel: (0)870 400 8134 Fax: (0)180 383 5040 General Manager: Kim Yardley
E-mail: HeritageHotels_Dartmouth.Dart_Marina@forte-hotels.com
Reservations: (0)870 400 8855 www.heritage-hotels.com

How to get there:

Motorists should take the A3122 from Totnes into Dartmouth. The road becomes College Way just before the Higher ferry, and the Dart Marina is on the left in Sandquay Road.

Facilities:
50 bedrooms with stunning views, room service, hairdryer, trouser press, restaurant, riverside terrace, bar, lounge, free car park.

Family:
Baby listening, baby sitting .

Leisure rates pppn

Midweek:	BB	DBB
Apr 2000	£ 50	£ 65
May–Jun	£ 60	£ 75
Jul–Sep	£ 70	£ 85
Oct–Nov	£ 60	£ 65
Dec–Feb	£ 45	£ 60
March 2001	£ 50	£ 65
Weekend:	**BB**	**DBB**
Apr 2000	£ 50	£ 65
May–Jun	£ 60	£ 75
Jul–Sep	£ 70	£ 85
Oct–Nov	£ 60	£ 75
Dec–Mar 2001	£ 50	£ 65

English Heritage Break rates

Validity dates: Tuesday to Saturday, November 2000– March 2001 £170 per person for a 2-night break. Based on two people sharing
Please quote 'Special Break'
when booking.

This part of England is forever linked with the name of Sir Francis Drake, England's famous seafaring hero who simply didn't recognise stress. He took time to finish his game of bowls and still beat the Spanish Armada. The theme of sea and sailing continues at the Dart Marina. All the bedrooms overlook the River Dart and the exclusive marina, as do the restaurant, lounge and terrace, which have superb views. Fresh fish landed at Brixham happens to be one of the hotel's many specialities. For an undisturbed view of the sailing craft, book one of the rooms with a balcony on the second floor.

English Heritage Break:

Arrive at your leisure at the Dart Marina to a Devon cream tea and check into your room with stunning views of the River Dart.

There will be a gift of local Dartington glass in your room to welcome you. A 3-course dinner will be served in Hauley's Restaurant featuring many fish specialities from Brixham quay, with a fine bottle of Chablis to complement the meal.

During your 2-day break you will have the opportunity to explore the historic town of Dartmouth, dominated by the Britannia Royal Naval College, and walk the many footpaths on the magnificent coastline. There will be complimentary tickets to both Dartmouth and Totnes castles, open between 10am and 4pm Wednesday to Sunday.

What's included in your break:
• 2 nights' accommodation in a room with a river view
• a gift of Dartington glass
• 3-course dinner in Hauley's award-winning restaurant each night
• a bottle of Chablis or wine of your choice with dinner each evening
• traditional English breakfast each morning
• Devon cream tea on arrival
• tickets to Dartmouth Castle and Totnes Castle

Dartmouth – Devon

1 Dartmouth

Wander the meandering streets, lined with half-timbered Elizabethan houses. Discover a wealth of individual art and antique shops. Explore the defensively positioned castle at the water's edge and the cobbled quay of Bayards Cove.

4 Dartmoor National Park

This vast expanse of wilderness is popular with ramblers, who scale its many hills and valleys. Pretty villages dot the landscape, but the real attraction lies in its natural isolation. Ponies that take their name from the moors can still be seen roaming freely in the area.

Local attractions/events:

Open all year (except some public holidays) unless otherwise shown

Dartmouth:

Museum: a 1640s merchant's building houses local history and events, particularly its maritime past
Britannia Royal Naval College: fine examples of historic artefacts in an imposing Edwardian building
Pottery Shop: unique setting of an architectural 'loft' in which to browse unusual arts and crafts or just enjoy a delicious snack/lunch served here
Dart River Cruises: sail up to the medieval town of Totnes, passing picturesque old towns and villages
Cheese & Wine Festival: The Dart Marina Hotel *(15-16 Apr)*
Folk Food: The Dart Marina Hotel *(4-6 May)*

Surrounding areas:

Cider Press Centre: *Dartington:* a village atmosphere which, in addition to cider tastings, offers a superb collection of Dartington Crystal, pottery, jewellery and traditional crafts
Torre Abbey, *Torquay:* Torbay's most historic building with a stunning picture gallery and an 'Agatha Christie' collection *(Apr-Nov)*
Bygones, *Torquay:* tread the paths of time, with over 20 shops and period rooms portraying different aspects and eras of the past
Paignton Zoo: now famous for the BBC1 series 'The Zookeepers'
Newton Abbot Racecourse: a convivial west country day out
Tuckers Maltings, nr Newton Abbot: your chance to become a Maltmaster and then sample some Real Ales *(Mar-Oct)*
Buckfast Abbey, *Buckfastleigh:* over 1000 years old, it is a 'living Benedictine Monastery'. You will be greeted by monks and observe them in their daily routines – making tonic wine or stained glass windows and bee-keeping are just a few examples
Buckland Abbey, *Yelverton:* the home of Sir Francis Drake, travel through 700 years of history in a day

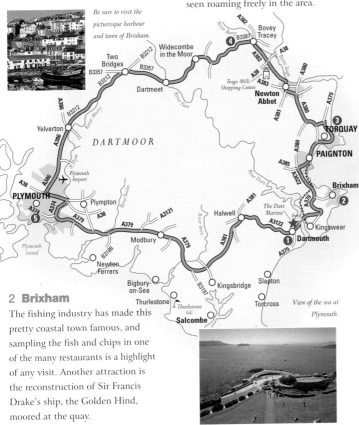

Be sure to visit the picturesque harbour and town of Brixham.

View of the sea at Plymouth.

2 Brixham

The fishing industry has made this pretty coastal town famous, and sampling the fish and chips in one of the many restaurants is a highlight of any visit. Another attraction is the reconstruction of Sir Francis Drake's ship, the Golden Hind, moored at the quay.

3 Torquay

Generally dubbed the 'English Riviera' because of its beachfront walks and mild climate, Torquay became a popular holiday destination in the 19th century, and is still packed with tourists. It was the setting for the classic British TV comedy Fawlty Towers.

5 Plymouth

Sir Francis Drake and other naval heroes made Plymouth their base for centuries, setting sail to defend their nation. The Mayflower Steps are another nod to history, as the sailing point for the Pilgrim Fathers on their way to the New World, and for Captain Cook's voyage to Australia.

73

Heritage Hotels – Dorking

The White Horse

High Street, Dorking, Surrey RH4 1BE *See map page 4*
Tel: (0)870 400 8282 Fax: (0)130 688 7241 Regional General Manager: Caroline Bellenger
E-mail: HeritageHotels_Dorking.White_Horse@forte-hotels.com
Reservations: (0)870 400 8855 www.heritage-hotels.com

How to get there:
To reach the White Horse, leave the M25 at junction 9, and take the A24 towards Leatherhead and Dorking. After four miles, take the third exit at the roundabout to Dorking town centre. Follow the High Street for 600 yards; the hotel is on your left.

Facilities: 69 bedrooms, 2 four-posters, 2 half-testers, hairdryer, trouser press, bar, restaurant, open fires in winter, free car park.
Family: Baby listening.

Leisure rates pppn

Midweek:	BB	DBB
Apr–Dec 2000	£ 84	£101
Jan–Mar 2001	£ 84	£101
Weekend:	**BB**	**DBB**
Apr–Dec 2000	£ 45	£ 55
Jan–Mar 2001	£ 45	£ 55

Special Break rates
Weekends only,
plus any 2 nights
19 July–28 August 2000
£150 per person for
two nights
*(Excludes Christmas and
New Year)*
Based on two people sharing
*Please quote 'Special Break'
when booking.*

With its old oak beams, open log fires and inviting lounge with nooks for quiet conversation, there is a positively Dickensian flavour about this beautiful old coaching inn. In fact, Charles Dickens was a visitor and did some of his writing here. The bedrooms feature two four-poster rooms, as welcoming as the restaurant with its traditional English menu. Dorking town has good shopping facilities and is great for antique hunting.

Special Break:
Arrive at the White Horse at your leisure in the afternoon. Check-in to your room and enjoy a cream tea in the fabulous lounge. A 3-course dinner awaits you in the restaurant.

Following breakfast, make your way to Denbies Wine Estate and enjoy a tour and wine tasting at this award-winning vineyard.Then, why not take a walk up Box Hill at your leisure?

After such an enjoyable day, the restaurant is again the setting for your evening dinner. Following a good night's sleep, breakfast is served before your departure. On your way home stop at Polesden Lacey to see this historic house.

What's included in your break:
• 2 nights' dinner, bed and breakfast
• champagne and flowers in your room on arrival
• 3-course dinner in the restaurant each night
• full English breakfast both days
• entry and wine tasting at Denbies Wine Estate
• entry to Polesden Lacey
• afternoon tea on arrival

Dorking – Surrey

1 Leith Hill

This hill to the south of Dorking, at 938 feet above sea level, is notable as the highest spot in Surrey. The stroll up the hill takes you through beautiful woodland. Tea and cakes are served from the folly at the top of the hill, Leith Hill Tower, where you can rest and enjoy the view.

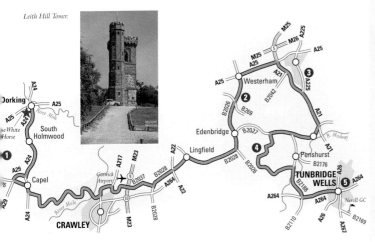

Leith Hill Tower.

2 Chartwell

English wartime prime minister Winston Churchill lived in this Tudor mansion from 1924 until 1965. The house has been preserved by the National Trust in his honour, and includes Churchill's fine collection of art and other personal effects. *(Mar-Oct)*

3 Knole House

This extravagant early 17th century house was commissioned by the Earl of Dorset, Thomas Sackville and the rooms are furnished with Sackville family memorabilia, including priceless rugs and tapestries. State rooms include a King's Room and a magnificent ballroom. *(Mar-Oct)*

4 Hever Castle

The 16th century childhood home of Anne Boleyn, Henry VIII's second wife, was restored in the early 20th century to its Tudor glory by the American millionaires, the Astors. The castle grounds are lovingly tended and as are much an attraction as the building itself. *(Mar-Oct)*

5 Royal Tunbridge Wells

The heyday of this spa town was in the 18th century, when high society would come here to take the restorative waters. Spring water can still be taken in the town's Bath House. *(Mar-Oct)*

Old colonnaded shopping street in Tunbridge Wells.

Local attractions/events:

Open all year (except some public holidays) unless otherwise shown

Dorking: *(also refer to page 59)*

Dorking & District Museum: an insight into the history of the local area

Dorking Halls: everything from musical events to Antique and Collectors' Fairs

Temptations: the largest selection of contemporary glass in Southern England

Surrounding areas:

Forge & Dragon Gallery, Forest Green: showing some extraordinary pieces of iron-art sited next to a fully operational forge

Winkworth Arboretum, Godalming: a hillside woodland with over 1,000 varieties of flora and fauna set around two lakes

Lingfield Racecourse: with as many 72 meetings a year, it can rightly claim to be England's busiest course

Gatwick Zoo, nr Crawley: a collection of rare and attractive animals, creating a 'near-natural' environment in large enclosures

Bocketts Farm, Fetcham: a working farm with the chance to taste some of the delicious home-made foods

Tonbridge Castle: travel back over 700 years and experience a vivid re-creation of the sights and sounds of 13th century life

Groombridge Place Gardens & Enchanted Forest, nr Tunbridge Wells: flanked by a moat, this classical 17th century manor has an intriguing history stretching back to medieval times *(Mar-Oct)*

Titsey Place & Gardens, Oxted: historic mansion house, extensive formal gardens, lakes, rose garden and Victorian walled kitchen garden *(May-Sep)*

Outwood Windmill, nr Redhill: England's oldest working windmill built in 1665. Museum of a bygone era *(Mar-Oct)*

Heritage Hotels – Dovedale

The Peveril of The Peak

Dovedale, Nr Ashbourne, Derbyshire DE6 2AW *See map page 8*
Tel: (0)870 400 8109 Fax: (0)133 535 0507 Regional General Manager: Debbie Johnson
E-mail: HeritageHotels_Dovedale.Peveril_of-the-peak@forte-hotels.com
Reservations: (0)870 400 8855 www.heritage-hotels.com

How to get there:
The village of Thorpe is just five miles north of Ashbourne on the eastern side of Dovedale. From junction 25 of the M1, follow the A52 for approximately 30 miles.

Facilities: 46 bedrooms, 2 four-posters, room service, restaurant, bar, lounge, free car park.
Family: Baby listening, baby sitting.

Leisure rates pppn

Midweek:	BB	DBB
Apr 2000	£ 39	£ 54
May–Jun	£ 45	£ 60
Jul–Aug	£ 52	£ 67
Sep–Nov	£ 45	£ 60
Dec–Feb	£ 39	£ 54
March 2001	£ 42	£ 57
Weekend:	**BB**	**DBB**
Apr 2000	£ 44	£ 59
May–Jun	£ 50	£ 65
Jul–Aug	£ 57	£ 72
Sep–Nov	£ 50	£ 65
Dec–Feb	£ 44	£ 59
March 2001	£ 47	£ 62

Special Break rates
April–October
£176 per person for 2 nights
November–March
£156 per person for 2 nights
Champagne and flowers package, £35 supplement.
Please quote 'Special Break' when booking.

The romantic-sounding Peveril of the Peak was named after one of Sir Walter Scott's novels. Most likely a local rectory in its original incarnation, it has been a hotel for about 100 years. Standing in 11 acres of terraced lawns, rockeries and grounds, it is surrounded by the splendour of the Peak District National Park and the superb walking areas of the White Peak area. Peak Practice was filmed here.

Peak Break:
Enjoy a 2-night stay at the Peveril of the Peak. The Hotel is situated at the edge of the Peak District National Park and is an ideal location to visit Alton Towers, Chatsworth House and Haddon Hall. On arrival in your room you will be welcomed with a posy of flowers and a box of Thornton's chocolates.
Day 1 – Explore the Treak Cliff Cavern and visit the gift shop. Upon your return enjoy a cream tea in the Chatsworth Lounge
Day 2 – Hire a bicycle for the whole day and take in the beautiful countryside on the Tissington Trail. The hotel will arrange for the bicycle to be delivered

to the hotel and will also provide you with a hearty packed lunch for your day out.

What's included in your break:
• free entry to the Treak Cliff Cavern
  (home of Blue John Stone)
• free cycle hire for the whole day and delivery to the hotel
• Thornton's chocolates and flowers in your room on arrival
• 3-course dinner each evening
• full English breakfast each morning
• afternoon tea – day one
• packed lunch – day two

Dovedale – Derbyshire

1 Peak District

The Peak District was England's first national park, established in 1951. The southern half of the park is the more aesthetic area, with limestone hills, wooded dales and pretty villages.

Stepping stones across the River Dove, in the Peak District.

2 Leek

Nicknamed 'Queen of the Moorlands' for its location on the edge of the Peak District, Leek rose to fame as the centre of the silk industry. Nearby is the 18th century Brindley Mill, built by the same engineer who masterminded the Bridgewater Canal.

3 Stoke-on-Trent

The name Stoke-on-Trent will forever be associated with the beautiful English pottery that was produced here from the end of the 18th century. Great names of the china industry, such as Royal Doulton and Wedgwood are still based here, and the small museum in the town recounts the history and offers examples for sale.

4 Burton-upon-Trent

British beer has many roots in this small town on the River Trent, and the Bass Brewery Museum tells its story, taking visitors through the brewing processes and offering much-needed tastings at the end of the tour.

5 Derby

Recognised for setting in motion the cogs of the Industrial Revolution, the city established the country's first factories and spinning mills. Royal Crown Derby celebrates its 250th anniversary and visitors can watch the fine china, tableware and giftware being made.

Potteries museum at Stoke-on-Trent.

Local attractions/events:
Open all year (except some public holidays) unless otherwise shown

Surrounding Areas:
(also refer to page 107)

Calke Abbey, *Ticknall:* no ordinary stately home but a fascinating mixture of spendour – and decay. A unique chance to see some eccentric collections in a great house with a walled garden, and parkland spotted with Red and Fallow Deer *(Mar-Oct)*

Creswell Crags, *Worksop:* famous limestone gorge with caves and lake. Earliest evidence of art in Britain, over 12000 years *(Feb-Oct)*

Pevril Castle, *Castleton:* breathtaking views of the Peak District from this castle, perched high above the pretty village *(Apr-Oct)*

Treak Cliff, *Castleton:* an underground wonderland of stalactites, stalagmites, rock formations and fossils. Home of the semi-precious gem, Blue John Stone *(Mar-Oct)*

Kedleston Hall, *Nr Derby:* this outstanding neo-classical mansion lies in a tranquil parkland setting with lakes, cascades and walks *(Mar-Oct)*

Derwent Valley Visitor Centre: see a Great Wheel, the Spinning Jenny and Crampton's Mole – the evolution of mechanical cotton spinning. Amongst other interesting exhibits, see the finest collection of hosiery from 1820-1920 *(Thur-Sun)*

Visitor Centre, *Denby:* jewellery, crafts and crystal ornaments, in addition to the more 'chunky' Denby pottery

Alton Towers: priding itself on terrifying rides, it is Britain's largest and most popular theme park

Well dressing: this strange tradition is found only in or around Derbyshire. It's thought to originate from water worship and is the art of decorating springs/wells with pictures made from 'growing things' and can be seen in various villages

Heritage Hotels – Dunster

The Luttrell Arms

32–36 High Street, Dunster, Somerset TA24 6SG *See map page 3*
Tel: (0)870 400 8110 Fax: (0)164 382 1567
E-mail: HeritageHotels_Dunster.Luttrell_Arms@forte-hotels.com
Reservations: (0)870 400 8855 www.heritage-hotels.com

How to get there:
The A39 North Devon coast road is the main route to Dunster. Turn south towards Tiverton on the A396. This is the Steep, which becomes the High Street. The hotel is on the left-hand side.

Facilities: 27 bedrooms,
4 four-posters, room service, hairdryer, trouser press, 2 restaurants, bar, lounge, open fires in winter, garden, pay car park.
Family: Baby listening, baby sitting.

Leisure rates pppn

Midweek:	BB	DBB
Apr–Jun 2000	£ 44	£ 59
Jul–Oct	£ 49	£ 64
Nov–Mar 2001	£ 44	£ 59
Weekend:	BB	DBB
Apr–May2000	£ 49	£ 64
Jun	£ 54	£ 64
Jul–Oct	£ 54	£ 69
Nov–Feb	£ 44	£ 59
March 2001	£ 49	£ 64

Special Break 1 rates
3-night (mid-week) break.
April 2000–March 2001,
£180 per person

Special Break 2 rates
3-night (mid-week) break.
November 2000–February 2001,
£155 per person
Please quote 'Special Break' when booking.

This is the perfect place for people trying to escape the frenetic pace of urban life. Here is a quiet, sleepy village (boasting one main street) in a perfect time warp. When dusk falls over this small 15th-century hotel, even the most prosaic guest might conjure up those medieval times when the Abbots of Cleeve used the Luttrell Arms as a guesthouse. Even insomniacs drift into easy slumbers amid this kind of tranquillity.

Special Break 1:
Arrive, check in and enjoy a welcome of champagne, chocolates and a book on Dunster Castle. Savour dinner each evening accompanied by complimentary house wine. Tickets to visit Dunster Castle are also included, and a light bar lunch on one day of your stay.

What's included in your break:
• champagne and chocolates in your room on arrival
• 3 nights' accommodation
• English breakfast
• 3-course dinner every night (*half bottle of house wine per person included every day*)
• a book on Dunster Castle
• entrance ticket to Dunster Castle

Special Break 2:
Arrive, check in and enjoy a cream tea at your leisure. A pre-dinner drink of your choice is included together with a bottle of house wine with dinner each night. A light lunch or cream tea will also be provided on the other days of your stay.

What's included in your break:
• 3 nights' accommodation
• English breakfast
• 3-course dinner every night (*1 bottle of house wine per couple included every day*)
• a pre-dinner drink of your choice

Dunster – Somerset

1 Dunster Castle

The small village of Dunster was the site of a Norman fortress, which operated as a military stronghold until the 17th century. The castle's interior has been restored to emulate its heyday, including a grand banqueting hall and bedrooms.

Exmoor has been affected by centuries of human activity but still supports a diverse range of flora and fauna.

2 Exmoor National Park

A popular way to explore this wilderness is on horse-back; various riding stables dot the landscape. Walking routes and classic English villages such as Winsford are further attractions. The area is also home to some rare wildlife, including the indigenous red deer.

The pretty town of Minehead is the start of the South West Way.

3 West Somerset Railway

Enjoy a nostalgic journey on a steam train through the unspoilt beauty of the Quantock Hills and along the coast, past Watchet Harbour, Blue Anchor Bay and Dunster. Any of the nine old-time stations are ideal for exploring the area. You can even dine on the train! *(Mar-Oct plus special event days)*

4 Coleridge Cottage

The poet Samuel Taylor Coleridge lived in this small cottage from 1796 in the small village of Nether Stowey, where he wrote his classic *Kubla Khan* and *The Rime of the Ancient Mariner.* The house preserves the poet's study and living room as they were during his lifetime.

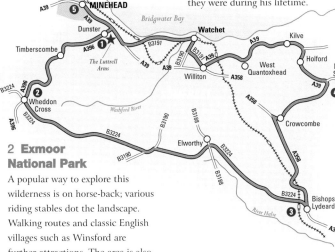

5 Minehead

A popular west country resort, it is the beginning of the South West Way, a 600 mile footpath that follows the coast of Devon, Cornwall and into Dorset. Along the route, various historical sights, spectacular views and indigenous wildlife delight walkers who take the path in summer.

Local attractions/events:

Open all year (except some public holidays) unless otherwise shown

Dunster:

Exmoor's Medieval Village: wander around and you will see why it has this reputation – the castle, rising above the main street, the working Water Mill and the ancient Yarn Market. A nationally renowned Museum of Dolls and an exhibition gallery for the Somerset Guild of Craftsmen also add to the sightseeing

A Celebration of West Country Cheese: The Luttrell Arms *(1-31 May)*

Classic English Puddings: The Luttrell Arms *(1-30 June)*

Surrounding areas:

Lynton & Lynmouth: where 'Exmoor meets the sea' – Lynmouth, with its picturesque harbourside is 900ft below its sister, Lynton, linked by a unique water operated cliff railway. The timeless beauty and romance of the magnificent coastline has drawn many 19th century poets to the area

Lyn and Exmoor Museum, Lynton: the 18th century cottage houses collections from this area, like Victorian kitchens, lifeboats, flood exhibits and railway *(Apr-Oct)*

Horsedrawn tours, West Ilkerton Farm: Shire horses pulling a purpose-built wagon – the more leisurely way to explore Exmoor *(May-Nov)*

Brass Rubbing & Hobbycraft Centre, Lynmouth: a popular family attraction with over 200 brasses *(Apr-Oct)*

Admiral Black Museum, Bridgewater: from stone axes to WWII ration books, medieval tiles to Victorian carnival posters, 19th century ship models to a video re-enactment of the battle of Sedgemoor – it's all here *(Mar-Oct)*

Somerset County Museum, Taunton: the castle and grounds have always been a focal point of Taunton's history, and you'll find many items of interest

Great British Heritage Pass 2000

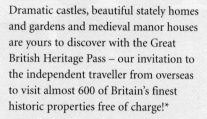

Dramatic castles, beautiful stately homes and gardens and medieval manor houses are yours to discover with the Great British Heritage Pass – our invitation to the independent traveller from overseas to visit almost 600 of Britain's finest historic properties free of charge!*

The handy pass gives you a rare opportunity to explore a wide variety of properties as described in your free gazetteer and located in whichever part of the country you are planning to travel. The National Trust, English Heritage, other heritage organisations and many privately-owned properties are all part of the pass.

How long is the pass valid and how much does it cost?

There are three types of passes available; a 7-day pass (£32)[†], a 15-day pass (£45)[†] and a 1-month pass (£60)[†].

[†]Or local currency equivalent.

For your free 2000 leaflet and order form please call your local BTA office:

*The Tower of London is half-price, all other properties give free entry with the pass.

BRITISH TOURIST AUTHORITY

Heritage Hotels – Exeter

The Southgate

Southernhay, East Exeter, Devon EX1 1QF *See map page 3*
Tel: (0)870 400 8333 Fax: (0)139 241 3549 General Manager: Tony Aspden
E-mail: HeritageHotels_Exeter.Southgate@forte-hotels.com
Reservations: (0)870 400 8855 www.heritage-hotels.com

How to get there:
Leave the M5 at junction 30, take the 3rd exit (Exeter and Dawlish). Take the 2nd left (signposted to the city centre) and the 3rd exit at the next roundabout. The Southgate is two miles further on at the end of the road.

Facilities:
105 bedrooms, 5 suites, 24-hour room service, mini-bar, hairdryer, trouser press, satellite TV, Cloisters Restaurant, bar, lounge, leisure club, including indoor pool, gym, saunas, solarium, whirlpool bath, free car park.
Family: Baby listening, baby sitting.

Leisure rates pppn

Midweek:	BB	DBB
Apr–Dec 2000	£ 60	£ 70
Jan–Feb	£ 60	£ 70
March 2001	£ 65	£ 75
Weekend:	BB	DBB
Apr–Jun 2000	£ 49	£ 64
Jul–Nov	£ 54	£ 69
Dec–Mar 2001	£ 49	£ 64

Special Break rates
Minimum stay of 3 nights – weekends only
May–October 2000, £195 pp
November 2000–March 2001, £170 pp
Please quote 'Special Break' when booking.

Exeter is an ancient, 12th-century Cathedral city and the Southgate, standing next to the Cathedral, succeeds in graciously blending the old and the new. This is a modern hotel, designed in Georgian style, built around the remaining four walls of a listed building. Sir Anthony Hopkins, who filmed The Remains of the Day at the nearby Powderham Castle, stayed here and enjoyed the hotel's sports facilities of indoor pool, gym and sauna. Fine walking near the Devon coast, Dartmoor and Exmoor.

Medieval Break:
Arrive at your leisure on Friday afternoon, settle into your room, come down and enjoy a traditional Devon cream tea in the lounge.
After breakfast on Saturday discover Exeter's heritage and enjoy a guided walking tour of medieval Exeter. Spend the afternoon exploring Exeter's big-name department stores and speciality boutiques. After all the activity during the day, relax over dinner in Cloisters Restaurant and enjoy a complimentary bottle of house wine per couple with your dinner.
On Sunday enjoy a trip north to Exmoor and the quaint village of Dunster, where lunch is provided at the 15th-century Luttrell Arms Hotel. Return to the Southgate Hotel in time for a rest or a refreshing dip in the pool before dinner in Cloisters Restaurant.

What's included in your break:
•3 nights' accommodation
•traditional Devon cream tea *(day 1)*
•English breakfast
•guided walking tour of medieval Exeter
•3-course dinner in the Cloisters Restaurant *(a bottle of house wine per couple included one day)*
•Sunday lunch at the Luttrell Arms Hotel in Dunster
•access to the pool

Exeter – Devon

1 Exeter

Exeter was a major city from its earliest days, first as a Roman settlement, then as a Norman trading centre. Statues in the cathedral commemorate early monarchs, such as Alfred and Richard II. Other medieval buildings abound in the city, including the 14th century Guildhall. The Quayside area has been renovated into an attractive setting for bars and restaurants.

3 Tiverton Castle

First built during the 12th century, Tiverton was largely rebuilt in the 14th century, hence its numerous medieval features. Today the castle has attractions such as secret passage tours, and medieval armour to try on. *(Apr-Sep, limited times)*

4 Sheppey's Cider Farm

Somerset is the home of English cider-brewing, and Sheppey's is a popular stop to see acres of apple orchards and sample the cider, which has been made here for centuries.

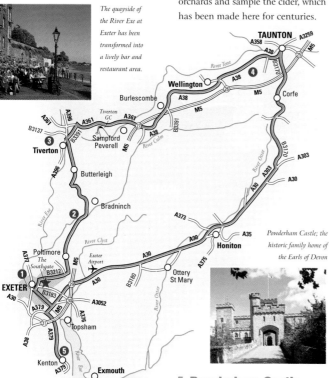

The quayside of the River Exe at Exeter has been transformed into a lively bar and restaurant area.

Powderham Castle; the historic family home of the Earls of Devon

5 Powderham Castle

This magnificent medieval fortress is set in an ancient deer park. There are lavish 18th century interiors in the state rooms, and wonderful gardens and grounds, including a Secret Garden containing friendly animals, especially for children. *(Mar-Oct)*

2 Killerton House

This 18th century former home of the Acland family, now headquarters of the National Trust, is needless to say, preserved along with many others to reflect its history and heyday.

Local attractions/events:

Open all year (except some public holidays) unless otherwise shown

Exeter:

The Cathedral of St Peter: completed in its present style by the end of the 14th century, its unique Norman twin towers dominate the skyline. It contains the tallest bishop's throne in England

The Royal Albert Memorial Museum: a wide range of displays, from local history and archaeology to showcases of world cultures

St Nicolas Priory: a former Benedictine Priory founded in 1087, visitors today can see the Norman undercroft and kitchen, the Tudor room with elaborate plasterwork and the grand guest hall *(Mar-Oct)*

Underground Passages: the only medieval subterranean aqueducts open to the public – a guided tour beneath the city centre with an exhibition and video presentation beforehand

Racecourse: set in the beautiful Haldon Hills, it has a year round programme of fixtures

Antiques Fairs: held at Matford Centre and Westpoint, with more than 500 stands at each event – at various times throughout the year

Classic Lobster: The Southgate Hotel *(8-21May)*

Brixham Fish festival: The Southgate Hotel *(12-25 Jun)*

Surrounding areas:

River Exe Cruises: these run from Exmouth and Topsham – stunning scenery and renowned wildlife on Britain's most beautiful river

Topsham: a once thriving port, it has a mixture of fascinating architectural styles, notably Dutch amongst the many antique shops, tearooms, pubs and restaurants. A visit to the Museum is also worthwhile

A la Ronde, *Exmouth:* an unusual folly of sixteen sides, it was designed by two women at the end of the 18th century – the staircase is covered with shells *(Apr-Oct)*

Heritage Hotels – Farnham

The Bush Hotel

The Borough, Farnham, Surrey GU9 7NN *See map page 4*
Tel: (0)870 400 8225 Fax: (0)125 273 3530 General Manager: Frank Harvey
E-mail: HeritageHotels_Farnham.Bush_Hotel@forte-hotels.com
Reservations: (0)870 400 8855 www.heritage-hotels.com

How to get there:
The Bush Hotel is at the lower end of Castle Street where it meets the A325 trunk route.

Facilities: 65 bedrooms, 1 four-poster, 3 mini-suites, hairdryer, trouser press, digital TV, restaurant, bar, lounge, free car park.
Family: Baby listening, baby sitting.

A favourite haunt for guests of this original 17th-century coaching inn is the candlelit, oak-beamed Coachman's Bar, where a log fire crackles in a centuries-old fireplace. In fine weather, guests make for the courtyard patio, with its tables perched on ancient cobblestones. The Georgian-style Thackery Restaurant serves traditional English dishes, and the lounge features atmospheric frescoes depicting historical scenes with – a rare oddity this – a sundial believed to reflect from the pond in the garden to tell the time. The Bush is mentioned in Thackeray's novel *The Virginians*. Great antique shopping and Murder Mystery Weekends.

Leisure rates pppn

Midweek:	BB	DBB
Apr–Dec 2000	£ 89	£106
Jan–Mar 2001	£ 89	£106
Weekend:	BB	DBB
Apr–Dec 2000	£ 45	£ 55
Jan–Mar 2001	£ 45	£ 55

Special Break rates

Weekends only, plus any 2 nights
21 July–30 August 2000
(Based on two people sharing)
£150 per person for two nights
Please quote 'Special Break' when booking.

Gardens Break:

Arrive at the Bush Hotel at your leisure in the afternoon. Check in to your room and enjoy a cream tea in the fabulous lounge. A 3-course dinner awaits you in Thackery's Restaurant. Following breakfast, make your way to Wisley Gardens and enjoy a gentle, or not so gentle, walk around the extensive grounds owned by the Royal Horticultural Society.
After such an enjoyable day, Thackery's Restaurant is again the setting for your evening dinner. After a good night's sleep, breakfast is served before your departure.

On your way home stop at Birdworld at Farnham to see the many exotic birds and many other attractions at this venue.

What's included in your break:
• 2 nights' dinner, bed and breakfast
• champagne and flowers in your room on arrival
• 3-course dinner in the restaurant each night
• full English breakfast both days
• entry to Wisley Gardens
• entry to Birdworld
• afternoon tea on arrival

Farnham – Surrey

1 Farnham

A town full of suprises – old and new. So what better way to discover its secrets than to follow the circular heritage trail? Take in the 12th century Castle, the Museum, Upper Church Lane and the Maltings - a few of the many sights to behold.

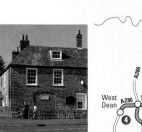

The Bush Hotel

3 Petworth House

This 17th century stately home is best known for its art collection, which includes works by the English artists Turner and Gainsborough. The beautiful grounds were landscaped by the master gardener 'Capability' Brown. *(Mar-Oct)*

4 Weald and Downland Museum

This open air museum, set in 50 acres of beautiful Sussex countryside, has a fascinating collection of over 40 regional historical buildings which have been rescued from destruction and carefully rebuilt to their original form, ranging from medieval to Victorian times. *(Mar-Oct)*

Chichester Cathedral.

Local attractions/events:

Open all year (except some public holidays) unless otherwise shown

Farnham:

Farnham Park: although evidence of actual dates refer to the Stone Age, its importance stems from the building of the castle in the 12th century, and it has had a fascinating history.

Coxbridge Farm: historic venue which includes tractor and trailer rides, horse and wagon rides, walks and rare animals

Festival 2000: six weeks of celebration – antiques, music, flowers theatre and much more *(10/6-22/7)*

Farnham Pottery: Victorian pottery established in 1872 *(Apr-Sep)*

Surrounding areas:
(also refer to pages 63 & 105)

Birdworld, *Holt Pound:* amazing birds in beautiful gardens, and many exotic species of birds and flowers *(Feb-Oct, weekends at other times)*

Manor Farm Craft Centre, *Seale:* an area of outstanding beauty, the old farm buildings display pottery, textiles, jewellery, glass and much more

Rural Life Centre, *Tilford:* museum of past village life set in 10 acres of woodland – it has a wheelwright's shop, a village smithy and an arboretum *(Apr-Sep)*

Selborne: famous for its association with the 18th century naturalist, Rev. Gilbert White, his house and gardens are open to the public, whilst the thatched cottages and 12th century church, pottery and exotic woodcrafts make it well worth a visit

Chichester: once a Roman town, it was elevated to city status with the construction of the 12th century cathedral. Today it is also noted for its arts festival in July

Jane Austen's house at Chawton.

2 Chawton

Towards the end of her life, the English novelist Jane Austen lived in this house and wrote two of her greatest works, *Pride and Prejudice* and *Sense and Sensibility* here. The house contains many of her belongings, including valuable first editions.

5 Goodwood

Goodwood House, like so many English stately homes, is a cornucopia of memorabilia collected by its owners over the last two centuries, including 18th century French furniture and an art collection that includes Van Dyck and Canaletto. Nearby is Goodwood racecourse, which includes a popular motor-racing circuit.

A Murder Mystery Weekend 'hotel – see pages 34-37

Heritage Hotels – Grasmere

The Swan

Grasmere, Nr Ambleside, Cumbria LA22 9RF *See map page 10*
Tel: (0)870 400 8132 Fax: (0)153 943 5741 Regional General Manager: Colin Campbell
E-mail: HeritageHotels_Grasmere.Swan@forte-hotels.com
Reservations: (0)870 400 8855 www.heritage-hotels.com

How to get there:
The Swan sits on the northern outskirts of the village of Grasmere, approximately halfway between Windermere and Keswick on the A591. Junctions 36 or 40 of the M6 provide access points.

Facilities:
36 bedrooms, 1 four-poster, 1 half-tester, hairdryer, trouser press, restaurant, 2 bars, lounge, open fires in winter, free car park.

Family:
Baby listening.

Leisure rates pppn

Midweek:	BB	DBB
Apr 2000	£ 50	£ 65
May–Oct	£ 54	£ 69
Nov–Feb	£ 35	£ 50
March 2001	£ 45	£ 60
Weekend:	BB	DBB
Apr 2000	£ 63	£ 78
May–Oct	£ 67	£ 82
Nov–Feb	£ 57	£ 72
March 2001	£ 63	£ 78

Wordsworth and the Lakes Break rates

Price per person for two nights

May–October 2000
Fri/Sat–£190
Sun/Thur–£165

November 2000–April 2001
Fri/Sat–£180
Sun/Thur–£145

Please quote 'Special Break' when booking.

A close neighbour of Dove Cottage, the Swan is a charming, old-fashioned hotel that prides itself on a true English welcome. Log fires burn in inglenook fireplaces – while in summer the hotel is an ideal base for an exploration of the Lakes.

Wordsworth and the Lakes Break:

Situated on the outskirts of the village of Grasmere, this charming inn nestles in the most spectacular scenery imaginable. Most bedrooms offer panoramic views of the fells through the Vale of Grasmere. In your room on arrival, champagne and Grasmere's famous gingerbread will be waiting. Dinner in the Waggoner Restaurant features the best of traditional cooking and reflects the awards gained in recent years.

After breakfast you have the choice of visiting either Dove Cottage or Rydal Mount. Dove Cottage was William Wordsworth's home for nine years, and next door is the museum which illustrates the poet's life with manuscripts, portraits and memorabilia.

Rydal Mount was the poet's home for 37 years and retains a lived-in family atmosphere with few changes and includes a four-acre garden much as he designed it.

After lunch an "eight lakes tour" is arranged, which takes you over Dunmail rise to Keswick and on to explore Borrowdale, Buttermere and Newlands valleys. Ascend both the dramatic Honister Pass as well as Newlands Hause. You will be driven alongside Derwent Water, Buttermere and see Crummock Water, before returning along the quiet west side of Thirlmere.

Dinner will again be four courses in the charming and hospitable environment that brings guests back time and again.

Breakfast prior to departure, with a last chance to explore before your journey home.

What's included in your break:
- 2 nights' dinner, bed and breakfast
  (wine not included)
- champagne and gingerbread
- tour of north lakes scenery
- entry to Dove Cottage and museum or Rydal Mount

Grasmere – Cumbria

1 Dove Cottage

Wordsworth's most famous Lake District home was in Grasmere itself. Here he wrote some of his finest work, as well as an early guidebook to the region he loved. A tour around Dove Cottage includes views of his original poetry manuscripts.
(Closed mid-Jan to mid-Feb)

Rydal Fell. The surrounding area was the home and the inspiration of one of England's greatest poets, William Wordsworth.

2 Rydal

One of William Wordsworth's homes in the region was Rydal Mount and the house, including the poet's study, has now been turned into a museum, documenting his life and work. The surrounding area in Rydal, like most of the Lake District, is very beautiful.

3 Derwent Water

One of many lakes from which the region takes its name is Derwent Water. The village of Borrowdale is one of the most attractive in the area. Lake cruises are available to take in the beautiful views.

4 Keswick

This 13th century town made its name by producing graphite, which was used as lead in pencils until the 18th century. Also near the town is the mysterious Castlerigg stone circle, dating back 4000 years and reminiscent of Stonehenge.

5 Cockermouth

The birthplace of William Wordsworth continues the tradition of its neighbouring towns by commemorating their greatest son. Wordsworth House is now a museum.

Local attractions/events:

Open all year (except some public holidays) unless otherwise shown

Surrounding areas:
(also refer to pages 139 & 143)

Lake Cruises, *Waterhead:* one of the many available for most of the larger lakes. Connects with other 'visitor attractions'. Evening wine cruises during the summer

The Teapottery, Museum and Art Gallery, *Keswick:* watch the unusual teapots being made by hand and learn some fascinating tea facts. The local Victorian Museum reveals Keswick's surprising past and some of its very famous residents *(Museum: Mar-Oct)*

Mirehouse House and Gardens, *Nr Keswick:* this historic house in a spectacular setting includes a walled honey garden, wildflower meadow and lakeside walks *(Apr-Oct)*

Cumberland Derwent Pencil Museum, *Keswick:* traces the history of pencil making from the discovery of graphite in the 1500s

Lakeland Sheep and Wool Centre, *Cockermouth:* witness the sheep being shorn (nearly 20 breeds) and sheepdogs at work

Jenny's Brewery Tour, *Cockermouth:* take in a tour, sample the brew and also visit the nearby Motor Museum *(Mar-Oct)*

Senhouse Roman/Maritime Museums, *Maryport:* the oldest collection of Roman sculpture and inscriptions in Britain displayed in an 1885 gun battery building adjoining the site of the fort built by the emperor Hadrian in 124 AD. The nearby Maritime Museum displays its proud heritage and connections with the Titanic and Fletcher Christian of *'Bounty'* fame

The Beacon, *Whitehaven:* situated on the harbourside of this Georgian town, it tells the story of the industrial, social and maritime heritage with audio visual displays

Avondale & Eskdale Railway: for over 100 years, steam trains have carried visitors from coast to hills

Heritage Hotels – Helmsley

The Black Swan

Market Place, Helmsley, North Yorkshire YO62 5BJ *See map page 11*
Tel: (0)870 400 8112 Fax: (0)143 977 0174 Regional General Manager: Gavin Dron
E-mail: HeritageHotels_Helmsley.BlackSwan@forte-hotels.com
Reservations: (0)870 400 8855 www.heritage-hotels.com

How to get there:
Helmsley is 15 miles to the east of Thirsk on the A170 in the direction of Scarborough. Sutton Bank, just before Helmsley, offers the driver

a true test of skill, and, reassuringly, caravans have now been forbidden from attempting this route.

Facilities: 45 bedrooms, 2 half-testers, hairdryer, restaurant, 2 bars, lounge, open fires in winter, free car park at the rear.
Family: Baby listening

The face of this small, 45-room hotel is a blend of Elizabethan, Georgian and Tudor – all of it charming, with warm, welcoming interiors of candlelight, oak beams and open fireplaces. Revelling in the friendly, family atmosphere, two members of staff have been serving in the Rutland Room Restaurant for a joint total of 97 years. You don't find staff like that any more!

Leisure rates pppn

Midweek:	BB	DBB
Apr–Nov 2000	£ 65	£ 85
Dec–Mar 2001	£ 50	£ 70
Weekend:	BB	DBB
Apr–Nov 2000	£ 83	£ 98
Dec–Mar 2001	£ 64	£ 79

Special Break rates

£235 per person for weekends
£195 per person for mid-week stays
Available April–October 2000
Please quote 'Special Break' when booking.

Special Break:

Arrive on your chosen day and settle into your room, which provides you with all the comforts you would expect from this well-appointed hotel. A bottle of champagne on ice and strawberries will be delivered to your room, providing you with the ideal excuse to relax and read the history of the Black Swan and the surrounding areas of Helmsley. As evening comes enjoy a full choice from the menu in the Rutland Room Restaurant, followed by coffee in one of the five lounges.
In the morning you will be provided with complimentary tickets to visit Castle Howard, home to the Howard family and the location used for the filming of *Brideshead Revisited*. In order that your day is uninterrupted you will also be given a packed lunch to enjoy at your leisure. You may choose to spend the full day exploring the stately home and its gardens or visit some of the many other places of interest mentioned within the Black Swan book.

On your second evening enjoy once again a full choice from the menu with time to reflect on all you have seen during the day.
The following morning there is no need to rush off. If possible you can check out late, giving you a last chance to walk around the town and buy some of the more unusual items that may not normally be available to you. Perhaps you may even be tempted to stay for lunch by the offer of two lunches for the price of one prior to your departure.

What's included in your break:
• 2 nights' dinner, bed and breakfast
• a bottle of champagne and strawberries in your room on arrival
• traditional English tea, scones and lashings of clotted cream each day
• a packed lunch *(day 2)*
• entrance tickets to Castle Howard

Helmsley – North Yorkshire

1 Helmsley

Rich in its own history, it lies beneath the protective gaze of an impressive 12th century castle, but it is also a pretty market town which lies on the edge of the North York Moors National Park. Nearby Duncombe Park is one of the finest restored houses in North Yorkshire. *(Apr-Oct)*

4 North Yorkshire Moors Railway

Beginning in the town of Pickering, this steam railway was constructed in 1835 and remains a popular tourist attraction. The 18-mile journey takes passengers through some of the finest moorland scenery. *(Apr-Oct)*

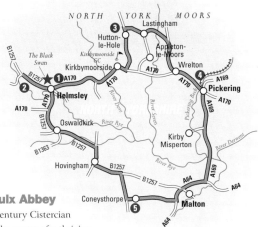

2 Rievaulx Abbey

This 12th century Cistercian abbey was the centre of a thriving community in its heyday, but its walls were destroyed in the 16th century. It is now in ruins, but the nearby terraces have wonderful views.

The 12th century ruined Cistercian abbey at Rievaulx.

3 Hutton-le-Hole

One of the most attractive villages in the north, Hutton-le-Hole continually buzzes with tourists, but nowhere else is there such a fine example of everyday Yorkshire moorland village life.

5 Castle Howard

Designed by Sir John Vanbrugh in the 17th century, the real attraction of this stately home is its setting for the television adaptation of Evelyn Waugh's 'Brideshead Revisited', fans of which flock here every year. *(Mar-Nov)*

The majestic Castle Howard.

Local attractions/events:
Open all year (except some public holidays) unless otherwise shown

Surrounding areas:

Rydale Folk Museum, *Hutton-le-Hole:* Yorkshire's leading open air museum, containing 12 buildings, all with displays, set in over three acres *(Mar-Nov)*

Cropton Brewery, *nr Pickering:* see, hear and smell how malt, hops and water are turned into seven real ales

Pickering Castle: one of the most splendid 12th century castles in northern England, featuring an 'English Kings' exhibition

Beck Isle Museum of Rural Life, *Pickering:* housed in a Regency mansion, it contains 24 rooms packed with collections from the Victorian era *(Mar-Oct)*

Eden Camp Modern History Theme Museum, *Malton:* a unique museum that transports you back to wartime Britain – the sights, sounds and smells of those dangerous times *(closed 24/12/00-10/1/01)*

Malton Museum: renowned for its rich archaeological collection, the imaginative displays are complemented by the Roman activity centre *(Mar-Oct)*

Nunnington Hall: this delightful 17th century house, with a lovely walled garden on a quiet riverbank, has remained in the same family for over 400 years *(Apr-Oct)*

York: just 27 miles away, this is possibly England's most historic city, with over 2000 years of history portrayed in twenty-eight attractions

Thirsk Racecourse: one of the many tracks to be found in Yorkshire

A Murder Mystery Weekend hotel – see pages 34-37

Heritage Hotels – Hertingfordbury

The White Horse

Hertingfordbury, Hertfordshire SG14 2LB *See map page 5*
Tel: (0)870 400 8114 Fax: (0)199 255 0809
E-mail: HeritageHotels_Hertingfordbury.White_Horse@forte-hotels.com
Reservations: (0)870 400 8855 www.heritage-hotels.com

How to get there:

Take the A414 to
Hertingfordbury and, on
reaching the village, turn
into Hertingfordbury Road.
The hotel is on the right.

Facilities: 42 bedrooms,
restaurant, bar, lounge, garden,
free car park.
Family: Baby listening,
baby sitting.

The Georgian façade of the White Horse actually belies a much older interior with oak beams dating back 400 years. Many of the spacious bedrooms overlook the hotel gardens, where lunch, drinks and a truly English tea are served in summer. In the grounds of nearby Hatfield House is the Old Palace, where Elizabeth I spent her childhood and learnt of her accession to the throne. The Old Palace is today the setting for regular Elizabethan banquets, providing insights into the lifestyle of the rich and famous centuries ago.

Leisure rates pppn

Midweek:	BB	DBB
Apr–Jun 2000	£ 75	£ 90
Jul–Aug	£ 65	£ 80
Sep–Mar 2001	£ 75	£ 90
Weekend:	**BB**	**DBB**
Apr–Jun 2000	£ 47	£ 62
Jul–Aug	£ 50	£ 65
Sep–Nov	£ 47	£ 62
Dec–Feb	£ 44	£ 59
March 2001	£ 47	£ 62

Special Break rates

January–June,
October–November, £115 per
person for two nights
Based on two sharing
*Please quote 'Special Break'
when booking.*

Special Break:

The White Horse, steeped in history and tradition and surrounded by countryside, is an ideal base to combine good food and comfortable surroundings with a visit to the Imperial War Museum, one of Britain's top aircraft and military museum attractions. Arrive and settle in before tucking into an afternoon cream tea in the lounge or, weather permitting, the delightful garden.

Enjoy a relaxing 3-course dinner with coffee in the Conservatory Restaurant, served with complimentary bottle of red or white Chilean wine, and round off the evening in the comfort of the lounge. Come down to a leisurely breakfast before setting off to Duxford, Europe's premier aviation museum

featuring the award-winning American Air Museum. Return and unwind with an aperitif in the bar before again enjoying dinner in the Conservatory Restaurant. Following breakfast, why not visit the Mosquito Aircraft Museum, a short drive from the hotel, before driving home?

What's included in your break:

- 2 nights' dinner, bed and breakfast
- a complimentary bottle of Chilean red or white wine per couple each evening
- afternoon cream tea on the day of arrival
- entry to the Imperial War Museum, Duxford
  (except on Airshow days)

Hertingfordbury – Hertfordshire

1 Hertford Castle

The administrative town for the county of Hertfordshire is dominated by its Norman castle, dating from the Norman Conquest of 1066. Another charm of the town is the many antique shops, which line its traditional streets.

2 Hatfield House

This Tudor mansion has a rich royal history, most notably as the house in which Elizabeth I was held hostage by her half-sister, Mary. The house thrives on its link with the Virgin Queen and includes many pieces of personal memorabilia within its richly decorated rooms. *(Mar-Sep)*

3 Knebworth

Many of the artefacts on display in this Tudor house are souvenirs from India, reminiscent of the fact that one-time owner Lord Lytton was the first Viceroy during the great days of the British Empire. Today the house is best known for the large-scale rock concerts held in its vast grounds. *(Mar-Sep)*

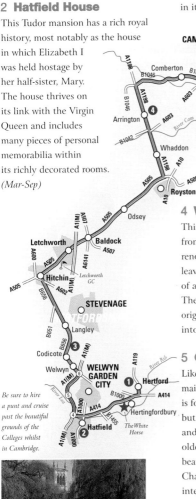

Knebworth House.

4 Wimpole Hall

This imposing mansion dates from the 18th century, but various renovations have taken place since, leaving the house a conglomeration of architectural styles. The servants' quarters remain original, offering a fascinating insight into life 'downstairs'. *(Mar-Nov)*

5 Cambridge

Like Oxford *(see pages 115/117)*, the main reason to visit this eastern town is for its ancient university buildings, but Cambridge tends to be quieter and less popular than its slightly older counterpart. One of the most beautiful sights is the King's College Chapel, with its 16th century interior and famed boys' choir, which performs each evening. Also like Oxford, the river plays a vital part in Cambridge life, and riverside pubs abound along the Cam's banks.

Be sure to hire a punt and cruise past the beautiful grounds of the Colleges whilst in Cambridge.

Local attractions/events:

Open all year (except some public holidays) unless otherwise shown

Surrounding areas:
(also refer to page 49)

Hertford Museum: extensive, century-old collections from the local areas in a 17th century town house with a recreated Jacobean knot garden *(Tues-Sat)*

Audley End House and Gardens, *Saffron Walden:* over thirty exquisite rooms containing fine pictures, silver and natural history collections *(Apr-Sep)*

Berkhamsted Castle: extensive remains of a once large castle with a complicated arrangement of inner and outer moats which can still be seen

Museum & Art Gallery, *Hitchin:* permanent displays in a late Georgian house include local history, a reconstructed Victorian chemist's shop, complemented by a garden of medicinal plants. The costume gallery presents over 200 years of fashion. Special exhibitions during the year

de Havilland Aircraft Heritage, *London Colney:* traces the history of aircraft development, particularly in this area, and incorporates the Mosquito Aircraft Museum

Bowman's Open Farm, *London Colney:* a working farm which gives you the chance to see and touch the animals *(Feb-Dec)*

Stondon Transport Museum, *Henlow:* Europe's largest private collection of cars, motorcycles, fire engines, army vehicles – and includes a full size replica of Captain Cook's ship *'The Endeavour'*

The Shuttleworth Collection, *Biggleswade:* world-famous collection of aircraft from Bleriot to the Spitfire, many appearing in regular displays between May and October

The Walter Rothschild Zoological Museum, *Tring:* once the private collection of Lord Rothschild, more than 4000 species of animals in a unique Victorian settting.

Champagne Perrier-Jouët
Timeless decadence for a nameless decade

Heritage Hotels – Kingston

Kingston Lodge

Kingston Hill, Kingston-Upon-Thames, Surrey KT2 7NP *See map page 4*
Tel: (0)870 400 8115 Fax: (0)181 547 1013 General Manager: James Lever
E-Mail: HeritageHotels_Kingston_upon_Thames.Kingston_Lodge@forte-hotels.com
Reservations: (0)870 400 8855 www.heritage-hotels.com

How to get there:
Kingston Lodge sits up on Kingston Hill, barely five minutes from the Robin Hood roundabout on the A3.

Facilities: 64 bedrooms, 1 four-poster, 2 mini-suites, hairdryer and trouser press in all bedrooms, restaurant, bar, lounge and free car parking.
Family: Baby sitting on request.

Leisure rates pppn

Midweek:	BB	DBB
Apr–Dec 2000	£ 90	£105
Jan–Mar 2001	£ 90	£105
Weekend:	**BB**	**DBB**
Apr 2000	£ 50	£ 65
May–Aug	£ 60	£ 75
Sep–Mar 2001	£ 50	£ 65

Special Break rates
Validity dates:
1 June 2000–31 March 2001
June–September 2000
£150 per person
October–December 2000
£130 per person
January–March 2001
£130 per person
(based on two people sharing)
Single supplement
£25 per person per night.
***Please quote 'Special Break'
when booking.***

The name has been deeply embedded in the history of the area for four centuries. It stands on the edge of one of London's greatest areas of greenery, Richmond Park, which has more than 2400 acres of parkland in which to ramble and perhaps share a quiet shady spot with a herd of Royal deer. The Lodge's bedrooms – one of which holds a four-poster bed – overlook Coombe Wood golf course or the flowers in the hotel courtyard. The Burnt Orange Restaurant offers an international selection of dishes.

Hampton Court Break:

Day 1 – Arrive at your leisure, check in to one of the recently refurbished rooms, and enjoy dinner in the Mediterranean surroundings of the Burnt Orange Restaurant overlooking The Courtyard Garden.

Day 2 – After breakfast, you are invited to visit Hampton Court with the hotel's compliments. This is England's finest royal palace, with over 500 years of history, and is situated on the banks of the River Thames. Follow in the footsteps of some of the greatest kings and queens through the magnificent state apartments, Great Hall and Chapel Royal. In the afternoon, a visit to Ham House at Petersham is recommended. An outstanding Stuart House built in 1610, Ham is famous for its lavish interiors and spectacular collections of fine furniture, textiles and paintings, as well as for the 17th-century formal gardens. Return to the hotel to relax with an aperitif in the lounge and reflect over dinner on the wonders of the day.

Day 3 – After a hearty English breakfast, check out of the hotel, and before you leave for home, wander around London's greatest park, Richmond Park. This 2400-acre parkland was created in 1637 by Charles I. Formal gardens blend with parkland where up to 700 fallow deer wander free. There is also Penn Ponds, Isabella Plantation, and an enclosed garden famous for its rhododendrons and azaleas.

What's included in your break:
• 2 nights' dinner, bed and breakfast
• ticket to Hampton Court
  (open every day except 24th–26th December. Mid-March to mid-October 9.30am to 6pm. Last admission 45 minutes before closing – normal ticket entry price £10 adult, £7.60 senior citizen)
• 3-course table d'hôte dinner menu
  (with coffee included)

Kingston – Surrey

1 Kingston

Both historic and royal – in fact the oldest of the four Royal Boroughs in England and Wales. Justifiably proud of its heritage, it is a superb example of a town with strong historical links successfully evolving into a thriving market town and, more latterly, renowned for its excellence as a shopping centre.

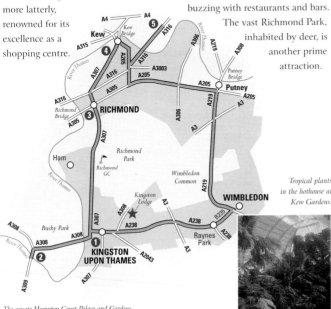

The ornate Hampton Court Palace and Gardens.

2 Hampton Court Palace

Home to Henry VIII and then Elizabeth I, Hampton Court is the finest Tudor palace in the country. The interior preserves the ornate state rooms, private apartments and works of art, as well as the 16th century kitchens. The grounds include a maze, ever crowded with lost and confused tourists.

3 Richmond upon Thames

Favoured home of the Tudor royal family, little remains of the former Richmond Palace, but the presence of royalty secured the position of this elegant town. The river lends it most of its character, the area around the bridge (London's oldest) buzzing with restaurants and bars. The vast Richmond Park, inhabited by deer, is another prime attraction.

Tropical plants in the hothouse at Kew Gardens.

4 Royal Botanical Gardens

These 18th century gardens are one of outer London's main tourist attractions. Most famous is the glass building of the Palm House in which various tropical plants thrive.

5 Chiswick House

Based on the designs of Italian architect Andrea Palladio, Chiswick House and its beautifully landscaped gardens were the centre of artistic society in the 18th century, entertained by the owner, the Earl of Burlington. *(Mar-Oct)*

Local attractions/events:

Open all year (except some public holidays) unless otherwise shown

Surrounding areas:
(also refer to pages 59 & 129)

Ham House, *Ham:* an outstanding Stuart house, built in 1610 and further enlarged in the 1670s, it is famous for its lavish interiors, collections of fine furniture, textiles and paintings *(Mar-Oct)*

Kew Bridge Steam Museum, *Brentford:* giant beam engines, the largest of their kind in in the world, operating under steam *(special events during the year)*

Museum of Richmond: covers many aspects of the area's history

Osterley Park House, *Isleworth:* set in 140 acres of landscaped park, Osterley was completed in 1575 but transformed in the mid-18th century by Robert Adam, creating a fine example of the 'grander lifestyle' of this period *(Mar-Sep)*

Claremont Landscape Gardens, *Esher:* its creation and development involved some of the great names in garden history, most notably 'Capability' Brown. Originally begun in 1715, the many features include a lake, an island with a pavilion, grotto, turf amphitheatre and marvellous vistas. Events take place here in the summer

Sandown Racecourse, *Esher:* flat and jump racing throughout the year

Brooklands Museum, *Weybridge:* the birthplace of British motorsport and aviation, exhibits include vintage cars, historic aircraft and other memorabilia plus the 24-litre Napier Railton, the greatest pre-war racing car in the world

Elmbridge Museum, *Weybridge:* newly refurbished, it has a permanent gallery on the history of the Elmbridge area

Syon Park, *Brentford:* London home of the Duke of Northumberland with magnificent Robert Adam interiors and a Great Conservatory in 30 acres of spectacular gardens *(House: Mar-Oct, Wed, Thu & Sat only)*

Heritage Hotels – Lavenham

The Swan

High Street, Lavenham, Sudbury, Suffolk CO10 9QA *See map page 5*
Tel: (0)870 400 8116 Fax: (0)178 724 8286 General Manager: Beth Raine
E-mail: HeritageHotels_Lavenham.Swan@forte-hotels.com
Reservations: (0)870 400 8855 www.heritage-hotels.com

How to get there:

The main A1141, off the A134 Sudbury to Bury St Edmunds road, runs into Lavenham itself, and the Swan is located on the main High Street.

Facilities: 44 bedrooms,

5 four-posters, 2 suites, 24-hour room service, hairdryer, trouser press, restaurant, 2 bars, 5 lounges, open fires in winter, free car park.

Family: Baby listening,

baby sitting on request.

Leisure rates pppn

Midweek:	BB	DBB
Apr–Aug 2000	£ 74	£ 94
Sep–Nov	£ 69	£ 89
Dec–Feb	£ 59	£ 79
March 2001	£ 69	£ 89
Weekend:	BB	DBB
Apr–Aug 2000	£ 89	£109
Sep–Nov	£ 84	£104
Dec–Feb	£ 74	£ 94
March 2001	£ 84	£104

Special Break rates

November 2000–March 2001
Mid-week from £200
per person (2 nights)
Weekends from £240
per person (2 nights)
Please quote 'Special Break' when booking.

Fully refurbished for the new millennium by an internationally renowned designer, The Swan provides some of Suffolk's most elegant accommodation. Medieval wall paintings were uncovered some years ago and influence the new decorations. The heart of the building remains untouched, with the half-timbered exterior and wooden beams marking one of the most admired periods of British architecture.

Special Break:

Lavenham is one of England's best-preserved medieval villages, situated in the beautiful countryside of Suffolk.

The Swan Hotel is found in the centre of the village and is renowned internationally for its excellent customer service and fine dining. Lavenham is the perfect base for exploring the University city of Cambridge, Colchester, England's oldest town, or Bury St Edmunds, famous for its abbey and gardens. Alternatively you may visit Kentwell Hall, Ikworth House, Melford Hall or Audley End. Why not visit the Swan for a unique experience and enjoy a romantic stay?

Before dinner, there is the chance to experience the history of Lavenham via an audio walking tour from the front of the hotel. Upon your return, enjoy a pre-dinner drink prior to your meal in the restaurant, accompanied by the resident pianist. The following day, enjoy a leisurely breakfast before

touring the area. In addition to the destinations already mentioned, to be recommended is a trip around '*Lovejoy Country*', including numerous antique shops, or reminisce at Flatford Mill or Dedham, where John Constable painted his famous landscapes. Upon your return, quench your thirst and appetite in the lovely surroundings before you again return to the comfort of your room.

After breakfast, spend a few moments in the spacious gardens and capture your memories on a postcard to your friends and relations before you begin your journey home.

What's included in your break:
• 2 nights' accommodation including dinner from the house menu and breakfast *(wine not included)*
• chocolates and flowers in the room upon arrival
• bottle of chilled Pommery champagne per couple
• audio tour of Lavenham

Lavenham – Suffolk

1 Lavenham

In the 15th century, England's wool trade was largely based in this village, and the residents have since carefully preserved its Tudor atmosphere. Buildings such as the Guildhall form part of what seems like a living museum.

This crooked house forms part of the "living museum" of Lavenham.

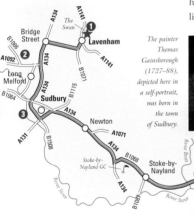

2 Kentwell Hall

The current owner of this 16th century mansion has lovingly restored it to is original glory, and takes visitors through life in Tudor times, complete with staff in authentic costumes speaking in archaic Tudor language. For anyone with an interest in this rich period of history, it should not be missed.

3 Sudbury

Two major artistic talents put this otherwise unassuming town on the map. In the 18th century it was the birthplace of the great English painter, Thomas Gainsborough, and his house has been preserved as a museum. The author Charles Dickens used Sudbury as the fictional setting for his humourous novel, 'The Pickwick Papers'.

4 Flatford Mill

This small house was the site from which the region's finest artist, John Constable, painted his most famous work, *The Hay Wain*. Nearby Bridge Cottage is now a museum devoted to the artist and his landscapes of English country life in the 19th century.

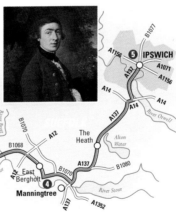

The painter Thomas Gainsborough (1727–88), depicted here in a self-portrait, was born in the town of Sudbury.

5 Ipswich

The centre of regional importance, today it offers a blend of history, character, maritime heritage as well as a wide choice of entertainment. Over the past years, a number of annual events have been organised to reflect its culture and ancestry, most notably – Maritime Ipswich, Orchestrelle, Charter Day and Music in the Park.

Heritage Hotels – Lincoln

The White Hart

Bailgate, Lincoln, Lincolnshire LN1 3AR *See map page 8*
Tel: (0)870 400 8117 Fax: (0)152 253 1798 Regional General Manager: Gavin Dron
E-mail: HeritageHotels_Lincoln.White_Hart@forte-hotels.com
Reservations: (0)870 400 8855 www.heritage-hotels.com

How to get there:
The White Hart is located in Bailgate, mid-way between the castle and the cathedral. The towers of the cathedral make a good landmark for new arrivals.

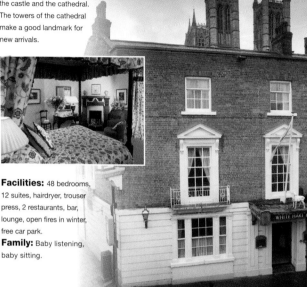

Facilities: 48 bedrooms, 12 suites, hairdryer, trouser press, 2 restaurants, bar, lounge, open fires in winter, free car park.
Family: Baby listening, baby sitting.

At the heart of the medieval city of Lincoln lies the White Hart, facing the overwhelming splendour of the ancient cathedral. The quaint cobbled streets leading up to the hotel, which was endowed with its emblem by Richard II when he stayed at the hostelry in 1372, are reminiscent of earlier centuries. There are mellow interiors with a fine collection of antique furnishings and, in the lounge, a collection of Rockingham china. Traditional English dishes are served in the King Richard Restaurant and the informal Orangery Bistro.

Leisure rates pppn

Midweek:	BB	DBB
Apr–Jun 2000	£ 60	£ 75
Jul–Aug	£ 50	£ 65
Sep–Mar 2001	£ 60	£ 75
Weekend:	BB	DBB
Apr–Jun 2000	£ 62	£ 72
Jul–Feb	£ 52	£ 67
March 2001	£ 62	£ 72

Golfing Break rates
Validity date:
Until 31 March 2001
2 nights £240 per person
3 nights £300 per person
Double or twin room for single occupancy carries normal hotel supplement.
Please quote 'Special Break' when booking.

Exclusive Golfing Break:
At the White Hart we are working in conjunction with the English Golf Union to offer you a short break and the opportunity of playing on one of the world's most outstanding courses. The Hotchkin course at Woodhall Spa was voted by Golf Magazine of America the 29th best course in the world – in 1999. The English Golf Union purchased the course in 1995. Since that time they have invested a large sum of money in creating one of the finest facilities in the world. They have built a second course, The Bracken, which although only two years old is of fine quality and has an American feel to its architecture. The Union has also developed extensive practice facilities, which include Europe's finest outdoors-short game training area. Indoors swing analysis can be conducted using the latest state of the art coaching equipment. Woodhall Spa is known as the National Centre for Golf in England and is a location which we are confident you will return to over and over again.

What's included in your break
• 2 or 3 nights' dinner, accommodation and breakfast, depending on your chosen length of stay.
• Upgrade to the best available room of its type.
• Three Heritage Hotel golf balls after your first day.
• £10 in vouchers to spend in the hotel bar.
• A free token for a set of practice balls for the driving range at Woodhall Spa.
• One round of golf on the world's 29th finest course, Hotchkin Course, Woodhall Spa.
• One round on the new Bracken Course.
• For parties of 12 or more, complimentary transport will be provided to and from the courses each day.
Members of English Golf Clubs may receive a discount off the above rates but will be required to provide a letter from their club secretary confirming paid subscriptions. NB: The offer is subject to availability of the courses that the hotel can make during your enquiry. Alternative courses will be sourced if the above are already reserved.

Lincoln – Lincolnshire

1 Lincoln

The spectacular towers of Lincoln Cathedral can be spotted for miles around and are the most distinctive image of the city. Nearby is Lincoln Castle, which houses one of the copies of the Magna Carta and a chilling prison display.

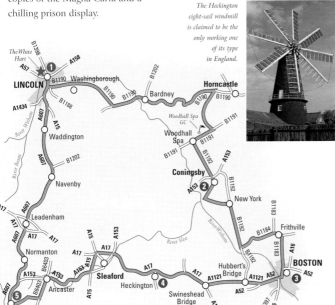

The Heckington eight-sail windmill is claimed to be the only working one of its type in England.

4 Heckington Windmill

Built in 1830, this eight-sailed windmill is still a working flour mill, grinding the corn solely by wind power. Flour made at the mill is on sale at the windmill shop.

2 Tattershall Castle

This magnificent 100ft high moated castle was built in the Middle Ages and restored in 1910 by Lord Curzon. The castle contains many preserved artefacts, including tapestries and furniture.

3 Boston

The familiar name of this attractive Anglo-Saxon town stems from the fact that the Pilgrim Fathers were arrested and imprisoned here when trying to escape to Holland. When they finally reached the New World, they named a new settlement after this Lincolnshire town.

The magnificent medieval Tattershall Castle.

5 Belton House

This grand, late 17th century house was built for a family of aristocrats who used their fortune to elaborately decorate their home, including some intricate limewood carvings. Family portraits by artists such as Reynolds line the walls.

Local attractions/events:

Open all year (except some public holidays) unless otherwise shown

Lincoln:

Castle: throughout the year a wide variety of events take place, such as craft fairs, historical re-enactments, jousting tournaments, medieval entertainment, brass band concerts and vintage car rallies
Museum of Lincolnshire Life: through a mixture of authentic room settings and changing temporary displays, this award-winning museum represents domestic, social and industrial life in the county over the past 200 years
Greyfriars Exhibition Centre: situated in a 13th century building, the exhibition for 2000 highlights the Saxon and Viking settlements
The Lawn: an extensive visitor attraction, it records the story of its origins as an asylum, historical and archaeological interpretations of the city, as well as providing the setting for the Banks Conservatory and the John Dawber Garden
Ellis Mill: standing majestically against the backdrop of the Cathedral, it dates from 1798 and is the sole survivor of a once impressive line of four-sailed windmills along the Lincoln Edge
City Cruises: discover the city from a relaxing, slow moving vessel along the River Witham *(Mar-Oct)*
Horse and Carriage: see Lincoln in Victorian style – a twenty minute drive around the Bailgate area *(summer only)*
Road and Transport Museum: vehicles from the 1920s to the 1970s, together with all sorts of memorabilia

Surrounding areas:

Old Hall, Gainsborough: an immaculately preserved 15th century manor house which has altered little since it was built; visitors get a real feel of life in a medieval household *(Mar-Oct)*
Racecourse, Market Rasen: racing fixtures throughout most of the year

Heritage Hotels – Marlow

The Compleat Angler

Marlow Bridge, Marlow, Buckinghamshire SL7 1RG *See map page 4*
Tel: (0)870 400 8100 Fax: (0)162 848 6388 Regional General Manager: Giorgio Borgonova
E-mail: HeritageHotels_Marlow.Compleat_Angler@forte-hotels.com
Reservations: (0)870 400 8855 www.heritage-hotels.com

How to get there:
The A404 dual carriageway links the M4 and M40 motorways. At the first roundabout follow signs for Bisham – the hotel is on the right immediately before Marlow Bridge.

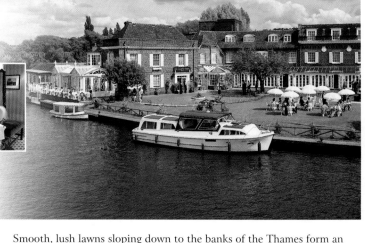

Facilities: 65 bedrooms, 2 suites, 5 four-posters, 24-hour room service, hairdryer, trouser press, satellite TV, restaurant, brasserie, bar, lounge, open fires in winter, croquet, riverbank fishing, summer boat trips, tennis court, gym *(walking distance)*, boat moorings, free car park.

Leisure rates pppn

All Week	BB	DBB
Apr 2000	£ 90	£110
May–Aug	£100	£120
Sep–Nov	£ 95	£115
Dec–Feb	£ 90	£110
March 2001	£ 95	£115

Wine and Boating Weekend rates
Validity dates: 28–30 July, 11–13 and 25–27 August 8–10 September
£259 per person
£25 single person supplement

A Taste of the Thames Weekend rates
Validity dates:
6–8 and 20–22 October
3–5 and 17–19 November
£259 per person
£25 single person supplement
Please quote 'Special Break' when booking.

Smooth, lush lawns sloping down to the banks of the Thames form an idyllic setting for this picturesque hotel with a spectacular view of Marlow Weir. The original 400-year-old bar still serves as a cosy drinking den, with open fires on chilly days. Take tea with freshly baked scones, preserves and clotted cream beneath garden parasols.

Wine and Boating Weekend:
Starting with a welcome cocktail party, enjoy a weekend of gourmet food, fine wines and some "messing about on the river".
Highlights of the weekend include a visit to the Old Luxters Vineyard on the slopes of Hambledon Valley for an exclusive tasting of their Chiltern Valley Wines, and the opportunity to explore one of the most beautiful stretches of the River Thames on a river cruise from the hotel's private jetty.

What's included in your break:
• 2 nights' accommodation
• cocktail reception
• 3-course dinners with half-bottle of wine (2 nights)
• English breakfast
• afternoon tea (*(Saturday)*
• visit to the Old Luxters Vineyard
• river cruise
(Transport to the vineyard and the river cruise are also included)

A Taste of the Thames Weekend:
After a welcoming cocktail party, explore life on the Thames from Isaak Walton to the present day: gourmet food, fine wines and the river's allure. Visit historic Henley on Thames and the "River and Rowing" Museum to experience the Regatta in its Edwardian heyday with all its regalia and even a full-sized steam launch. Meander along the banks of the river and enjoy a taste of England with full-bodied Chiltern Valley Wines from the Old Luxter Vineyard on the slopes of Hambledon Valley.

What's included in your break:
• 2 nights' accommodation
• cocktail reception and introductory talk
• 3-course dinner with half-bottle of wine (2 nights)
• English breakfast
• afternoon tea (Saturday)
(Transport and entrance to the museum and the vineyard are included)

Marlow – Buckinghamshire

1 Marlow

A Georgian town, situated on a beautiful stretch of the River Thames, an ideal location to see the natural beauty of the Chiltern Hills. Of some architectural and historical interest, Marlow is most noted for its 19th century suspension bridge, designed by Tierney Clarke, similar to the one over the River Danube in Budapest.

4 Henley-on-Thames

Prettily located on the Thames, with a famous bridge built in 1786, Henley is dominated by the 13th century St Mary's Church with its 16th century flint tower. One of England's many grand occasions is the Henley Royal Regatta, a rowing competition that takes place at the end of June.

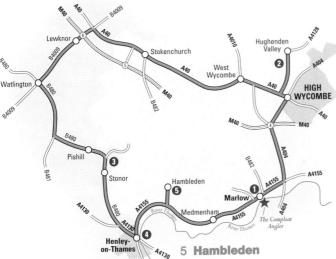

2 Hughenden Manor

The home of the 19th century prime minister Benjamin Disraeli is open to the public and preserves the rooms in their Victorian glory. The house is set in beautifully landscaped gardens and extensive parkland.

3 Stonor Park

Although most of this ancestral home dates from the 14th century, with later additions to the façade, there is evidence that a smaller house existed here as early as 1190. Sir Edmund Campion used the house as a refuge while writing his *Decem Rationes*, and Stonor now includes an exhibition about his life.

5 Hambleden

Situated in one of the prettiest Chiltern valleys, this is a village where time seems to have stopped. Lord Cardigan (of *'Light Brigade'* fame) was born in the Manor House and his sea-chest is preserved in the beautiful old church. Nearby stands Hambleden Mill, a strategic point on the Thames, with the original weir dating back to 1420.

The beautifully landscaped grounds of Stonor Park.

Heritage Hotels – Matlock Bath

The New Bath Hotel

New Bath Road, Matlock Bath, Derbyshire DE4 3PX *See map page 8*
Tel: (0)870 400 8119 Fax: (0)162 958 0268 Regional General Manager: Debbie Johnson
E-mail: HeritageHotels_Bath.Matlock.New_Bath@forte-hotels.com
Reservations: (0)870 400 8855 www.heritage-hotels.com

How to get there:

From the M1 leave at junction 28. Follow the signs to Matlock along the A38. Turn off at the A610 and follow signs to Ambergate. Turn right at the A6 towards Matlock. The hotel is on the left-hand side just before you reach Matlock Bath.

Facilities: 55 bedrooms, 8 half-testers, 2 four-posters, hairdryer, trouser press, restaurant, bar, lounge, open fires in winter, tennis court, indoor heated plunge pool, sauna, solarium, thermal-fed outdoor pool, free car park.
Family: Baby listening, baby sitting, children's play area.

Matlock Bath first became recognised in Regency times for its medicinal springs. The New Bath Hotel was built in 1802 and boasts an outdoor pool and an indoor heated plunge pool, both fed by natural springs. The old mining area has become a tourist attraction and the Heights of Abraham is popular for the cable car that runs high above the town to Victoria Tower and the mining shafts. Sailing and golf are found locally.

Leisure rates pppn

Midweek:	BB	DBB
Apr–Jun 2000	£ 55	£ 70
Jul–Aug	£ 60	£ 75
Sep–Nov	£ 50	£ 65
Dec–Feb	£ 45	£ 60
March 2001	£ 50	£ 65
Weekend:	BB	DBB
Apr–Jun 2000	£ 59	£ 74
Jul–Aug	£ 64	£ 79
Sep–Nov	£ 54	£ 69
Dec–Feb	£ 49	£ 64
March 2001	£ 54	£ 69

Pottery and Bone China Break rates

April 2000–March 2001
£175 per person for 2 days
Please quote 'Special Break' when booking.

Pottery and Bone China Break:

On arrival in your room you will find a complimentary box of Thornton's chocolates and a posy of flowers.

A tour and demonstration is offered around the museum and factory shop at the celebrated Royal Crown Derby Centre.

Also included is a fully guided tour of the Derby Pottery Visitors Centre

Upon your return each day you will be able to enjoy a cream tea in the Spinners Lounge at your leisure. What's included in your break:

• entry to the Royal Crown Derby Centre
• entry to the Denby Pottery Visitors Centre
• Thornton's chocolates and flowers in your room on arrival
• 3-course dinner each evening
• full English breakfast each morning
• afternoon tea each day

Matlock Bath – Derbyshire

1 The Heights of Abraham

The cable car or the caverns – just two of the attractions in this Country Park. Take a ride high above the river and gorge to the summit or join a guided tour down two famous caverns, which include a dramatic multivision presentation.

2 Haddon Hall

This is one of the finest medieval manor houses in England. Features include wall paintings in the chapel, traditional medieval kitchens and a Long Gallery. The house was used as the location of Rochester's home in the film adaptation of 'Jane Eyre'.

4 Buxton

Romans were the first to discover the fresh spring water of this town, which is now exported around the world. The Regency architecture in Buxton is a result of the 18th century passion for spa towns.

5 Chatsworth House

The traditional home of the Duke of Devonshire was built in the 17th century. A highlight of the interior is the elaborate dining room, where the table setting is exactly as it was for the visiting King George V in 1933. The spectacular gardens were designed by 'Capability' Brown.

Chatsworth House in autumn.

3 Bakewell

This attractive town on the River Wye is home to the traditional Bakewell Pudding, a sweet almond pie misnamed as the Bakewell Tart. The pie is still made here, much to the delight of visitors who purchase huge quantities.

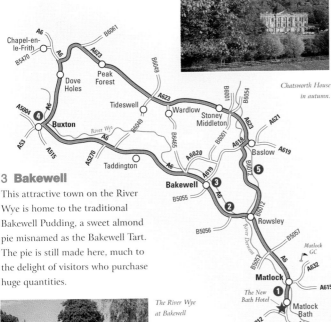

The River Wye at Bakewell

Local attractions/events:

Open all year (except some public holidays) unless otherwise shown

Matlock Bath/Matlock:

Peak Rail: steam trains operate on this track, and you can even enjoy a meal aboard (all week June-Aug, weekends other times)

National Tramway Museum: vintage tram rides on Period Street, plus other attractions (Apr-Oct)

Surrounding areas:
(also refer to page 77)

Caudwell's Mill, Rowsley: Victorian turbine powered roller flour mill with original machinery (Mar-Oct)

Wind in the Willows, Rowsley: a new attraction dedicated to this classic adventure story (Jun-Sep)

Poole's Cavern, Buxton: natural cavern with spectacular chambers, stalagmites and crystal formations (Mar-Oct)

Museum, Buxton: discover the geology, archaeology and history of the Peak District

Egham Hall and Museum: delightful 17th century family home with tapestries, portraits and costumes collected over three centuries. As well as other local history, it documents the Bubonic Plague in 1665/6 and its effect on the area

Chesterfield: this has much to offer – the Market, the Crooked Spire of St Mary and All Saints (leans 9' 5" from its true centre) and the Museum, which records history from Roman times to the present day

Bolsover Castle: enchanting castle, high on a wooded hilltop, with elaborate fireplaces, panelling and wall paintings (Apr-Oct)

Pennine Way: a 250 mile route to Scotland begins at Edale – but most visitors walk only part of the route.

A Music at Leisure Weekend hotel – see pages 32-33
A Murder Mystery Weekend hotel – see pages 34-37

Heritage Hotels – Mudeford

The Avonmouth Hotel

Mudeford, Christchurch, Dorset BH23 3NT *See map page 4*
Tel: (0)870 400 8120 Fax: (0)120 247 9004 Regional General Manager: Adam Terpening
E-mail: HeritageHotels_Mudeford_Christchurch.Avonmouth@forte-hotels.com

How to get there:

From the North of the A46 ring road, follow the brown tourist signs for the cathedral. At Newport Arch, part of the ancient walls of the city, turn right for the Bailgate shopping area, go through the arch and

follow the narrow one way street until you reach the left-hand turn. The hotel is located in front of you.

Facilities: 40 bedrooms

(14 located in separate ground-floor wing with estuary views), room service, hairdryer, trouser press, restaurant and bar overlooking the estuary, 2 lounges *(1 non-smoking)*, heated outdoor pool *(June–August)*, croquet lawn, junior putting green, free car park.

Family: Baby listening,

baby sitting, games room (July–August).

Leisure rates pppn

Midweek:	BB	DBB
April	£ 54	£ 64
May–June	£ 59	£ 64
July–Aug	£ 69	£ 79
Sep–Nov	£ 54	£ 69
Dec–Mar 2001	£ 44	£ 54
Weekend:		
April	£ 54	£ 69
May–June	£ 59	£ 69
July–Aug	£ 69	£ 79
Sep–Nov	£ 54	£ 69
Dec–Mar 2001	£ 44	£ 59

Please quote 'Special Break' when booking.

The hotel, built in the 1820s, is set in extensive grounds with stunning views of the Christchurch estuary, Mudeford Quay and the dramatic Hengistbury Head. One feature of the hotel is the Orchard Wing bedrooms; here you can make the most of individual private patios, reserved parking and magnificent views. Rooms in the main house also have fine views across the estuary, and the hotel also has an outdoor heated swimming pool. The surrounding area is rich in conservation, with mudflats and marshes offering promising exploration and ornithological opportunities. The Harbour View restaurant offers a relaxed atmosphere in which to dine and enjoy the award winning food.

Special Break 1:

Arrive to a warm welcome and check in and enjoy your comfortable bedroom with a complimentary box of chocolates. A ticket to Beaulieu with its house, grounds and, of course, the famous motor museum is available for you to use during your stay. (Closed during December)

What's included in your break:
• 2 nights' dinner, bed and breakfast
• complimentary box of chocolates
• ticket for Beaulieu

Special Break 2:

Arrive to a warm welcome, check in and enjoy a complimentary bottle of Pommery champagne. A ticket to Marwell Zoo is available for you to use during your stay. Here you can see how the animal conservation programme is developing and even adopt an animal.

What's included in your break:
• 2 nights' dinner, bed and breakfast
• complimentary bottle of champagne
• ticket for Marwell

Mudeford – Dorset

1 Christchurch

Just 2 miles from Mudeford, Christchurch has a lot to offer, especially the older part of the town with the magnificent Priory Church, Red House Museum and Place Mill, all illustrating the fascinating heritage of this ancient borough. Beaches also abound, as well as being a natural harbour and fishing haven.

2 Wimborne Minster

The town is named in honour of its ancient and impressive church, which has numerous Norman details. The church's library is one of the oldest in the country, dating from 1686.

4 Corfe Castle

This ancient castle suffered cruelly at the hands of the Roundheads during the English Civil War. They ousted the Royalist Bankes family, who then moved to Kingston Lacy. Reduced to ruins by the attack, the castle remains a popular visitor attraction.

The town of Corfe Castle, which takes its name from the ruined castle on the hill behind.

The Avonmouth Hotel

The unusual rock formation of Durdle Door.

3 Kingston Lacy

A 17th century stately home, worth visiting for its art collection, including works by Rubens. Another room houses souvenirs from the 19th century travels of the home's then owner, William Bankes.

5 Durdle Door

One of southern England's most photographed sights is this limestone arch jutting out from the bay. Nearby is another tourist hotspot, the semi-circular Lulworth Cove.

Local attractions/events:

Open all year (except some public holidays) unless otherwise shown

Surrounding areas:
(also refer to page 127)

Christchurch Priory: reputed to be the largest Parish church in England, it has a Norman nave dating back to 1094, the Miraculous Beam (a ninth centenary commemorative stained glass window) and a restored 18th century organ

Place Mill, *Christchurch:* a restored Anglo-Saxon water mill, uniquely situated at the confluence of the Rivers Stour and Avon

Red House Museum and Gardens, *Christchurch:* countless interesting objects, local history, geology, natural history and archaeology form just some of the exhibitions

Harbour Cruises: a great way to see the coastal area, including the Mudeford Sandbank

Southern Electric Museum, *Christchurch:* set in a genuine Edwardian power station, it displays many early domestic items, as well as more unusual uses for electricity, like the 40ft long Dreadnought Tram *(Mar-Sep)*

Highcliffe Castle: within cliff top grounds, it has exhibitions and events throughout the season *(May-Oct)*

Bournemouth: one of Britain's most popular seaside resorts, with a long sandy beach and plenty to see and do. The romantic poet Shelley lived here, and a museum holds his personal belongings as well as those of his wife, Mary, who wrote the novel *'Frankenstein'*

Aviation Museum, *Bournemouth:* an operational base where ex-military vintage aircraft such as Hunters, Vampires and Venoms are restored and flown

Tank Museum, *Bovington:* houses the world's finest collection of Armoured Fighting Vehicles

A Murder Mystery Weekend hotel – see pages 34-37

Heritage Hotels – North Berwick

The Marine

Cromwell Road, North Berwick, East Lothian EH39 4LZ *See map page 13*
Tel: (0)870 400 8129 Fax: (0)162 089 4480 Regional General Manager: Joe Longmuir
E-mail: HeritageHotels_Berwick.Marine@forte-hotels.com
Reservations: (0)870 400 8855 www.heritage-hotels.com

How to get there:
From the A198, Dirleton Avenue, turn into Hamilton Road and take the second right into Cromwell Road.

Facilities: 83 bedrooms including 6 four-posters, 5 suites and 4 mini-suites, hairdryer, trouser press, restaurant, bar, lounge, Leisure Club includes heated outdoor pool (May–October), sauna, solarium, table-tennis, 2 tennis courts, putting green, snooker, gardens, hairdresser, free car park.
Family: Baby listening, children's playground, nursery.

The Marine Hotel is a gloriously embellished example of Victoriana, picturesquely located at the heart of East Lothian's golfing coast. The Marine actually overlooks the 16th green of North Berwick's championship West Links course, which threads along the edge of the Firth of Forth and includes one of golf's most-copied holes, the infamous 15th "Redan". Real golf afficionados should take one of the 40 sea view rooms and suites at the rear, where they can watch players tackling several holes of the West Links course from dawn to dusk.

Leisure rates pppn

All Week	BB	DBB
Apr 2000	£ 45	£ 60
May–Jun	£ 55	£ 70
Jul–Aug	£ 65	£ 80
Sep–Nov	£ 55	£ 70
Dec–Mar	£ 45	£ 60

Special Break rates

£20 per person per night extra
Validity date: any day from June 2000–March 2001
Please quote 'Special Break' when booking.

Golf Inclusive Break:

Our Golf Inclusive Break offers a Welcome Golf Pack, 3 balls and a towel plus one round of golf per day at the Whitekirk golf course for only an extra £20 per person per day. Situated 3 miles east of North Berwick, the course has commanding views over East Lothian and beyond. Hosting the televised Professional MasterCard East Lothian Classic in 1999 put Whitekirk on the map – and the Classic will be returning again in 2000. Whitekirk also has an excellent 300-yard practice range.

What's included in your break:
• a Welcome Golf Pack, 3 balls and a towel
• a round of golf per day at the Whitekirk golf course.

North Berwick – East Lothian

1 North Berwick

Made a Royal Burgh in 1373 by King Robert II, it became a popular destination in Victorian times with the opening of the railway. Just half an hour away from Scotland's capital, Edinburgh, it offers visitors a healthy alternative with plenty of places to walk for breathtaking cliff top views, like the North Berwick Law, a 612ft hill, or the ruins of the 14th century Tantallon Castle. Venture inland and you'll discover numerous picturesque villages.

The ruined Tantallon Castle is an evocative sight, perched as it is at the edge of a cliff.

2 Bass Rock

A ferry from North Berwick takes visitors to this island rock, which has now been turned into a bird sanctuary. Gannets, puffins and cormorants are among the species that can be seen here.

3 Haddington

Traditionally a farming town, the appeal of Haddington today lies in its 17th and 18th century houses, whose architectural features include ornamental gables and towers.

4 Edinburgh

The capital of Scotland is an attractive city built on an extinct volcano and with a rich past. One of the most popular sights is the castle on top of the mound, which dates from the 12th century. The city is always busy, but it is crammed to bursting twice a year – during the popular arts festival in August and for Scotland's lively Hogmanay celebrations each New Year's Eve.

Firework celebrations at the Edinburgh festival.

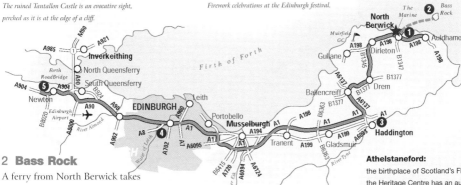

5 Hopetoun House

The finest stately home in Scotland, Hopetoun House was built in the 18th century in a grand Baroque style. Art and tapestries are on display inside, and the grounds, with their riverside setting, are a popular resting spot.

Local attractions/events:

Open all year (except some public holidays) unless otherwise shown

Surrounding areas:

Museum of Flight, *nr Haddington:* this National Museum of Aviation, set in airfield hangars, has a massive collection of aircraft and related items

Fenton Barns Retail & Leisure Village, *nr North Berwick:* this has been created with the specific aim of providing a range of high quality goods and services with the emphasis on traditional values

Scottish Archery Centre: test your archery or crossbow skills in this indoor centre, all under supervision and instruction

Myreton Motor Museum, *Aberlady:* a collection of cars and other motor vehicles from 1896, together with period advertising – posters, enamel signs and so on

Athelstaneford: the birthplace of Scotland's Flag, the Heritage Centre has an audio visual dramatisation of its tradition and origin *(Apr-Sep)*

Glenkinchie Distillery Visitor Centre, *Tranent:* a working distillery producing one of the highly acclaimed malts, a sample of which you can taste after an informative tour *(Apr-Nov)*

Scottish Mining Museum, *Newtongrange:* this record breaking colliery has Scotland's largest steam engine and records 'the hardest work under heaven' *(Mar-Nov)*

Heritage Hotels – Oxford

The Eastgate

The High Street, Oxford OX1 4BE *See map page 4*
Tel: (0)870 400 8201 Fax: (0)186 579 1681 Regional General Manager: James Stewart
E-mail: HeritageHotels_Oxford.Eastgate@forte-hotels.com
Reservations: (0)870 400 8855 www.heritage-hotels.com

How to get there:
The Eastgate is situated right in the very heart of central Oxford on the High Street.

Facilities: 63 bedrooms, 1 mini-suite with four-poster, 24- hour room service, hairdryer, trouser press, restaurant, bar, lounge, car park £10 per 24 hours.
Family: Baby listening, baby sitting.

Leisure rates pppn

Midweek:	BB	DBB
Apr–Jun 2000	£ 75	£ 85
Jul–Aug	£ 65	£ 75
Sep–Nov	£ 75	£ 85
Dec–Feb	£ 65	£ 75
March 2001	£ 75	£ 85
Weekend:	BB	DBB
Apr 2000	£ 80	£ 90
May–Jun	£ 85	£ 95
Jul–Aug	£ 70	£ 80
Sep–Nov	£ 80	£ 90
Dec–Feb	£ 70	£ 80
March 2001	£ 80	£ 90

Bohemian Oxford Break rates

Validity dates: all dates until March 2001
£155 per person for a 2-night break (based on two people sharing. Wine not included with meals)
Please quote 'Special Break' when booking.

Originally a 17th-century coaching inn, the hotel has had recent renovations that remain in keeping with the mellow architecture of the city. It is situated right in the centre of the town, and Magdalen College is a near neighbour. Tours of the colleges are easily arranged. In turn, Oxford students have quite taken to the hotel's lively Café Boheme, a French-style brasserie providing jazz in the afternoon. A sister bar, also Bohemian in character, serves coffee and drinks. There's punting on the river and good shopping in Oxford.

Bohemian Oxford Break:

The new Café Boheme Restaurant is the sister to the Café Boheme in Soho, London. It is a lively restaurant and bar with a mix of students, artists and the local café society. Most evenings live jazz is played and it is a wonderful place to sit and watch Oxford unfold.

Choose a 3-course meal from the extensive menu and stay a while to soak up the atmosphere of the bar, which is open until 1am each night.

The next morning, Café Boheme is the setting for breakfast with probably the best cappuccino in town. Entry is organised into the Oxford Story attraction, which transports you through 800 years of the university. This is only a 10-minute walk from the hotel.

A book of discount vouchers for some of the Bicester Village discount retail outlets is included, which offers between 10% and 35% discount on various designer labels (e.g. Racing Green, Versace, Calvin Klein) – 25 minutes' drive from the hotel.

Following breakfast the next morning, before departing you might like to take a tour of one of the colleges.

What's included in your break:
• 2 nights' accommodation
• 2 dinners in Café Boheme
• 2 breakfasts in Café Boheme
• entry to the Oxford Story
• discount vouchers for Bicester Village

Oxford – Oxfordshire

1 The Oxford Story

An excellent introduction to Oxford. Step aboard this amazing 'ride' and enjoy a fascinating journey of discovery spanning 800 years. From scientists to politicians, poets to comedians and the men and women of Oxford University who have made their mark on history.

2 Burford

The idyllic setting of this town, on the banks of the river Windrush, is typical of the Cotswolds area. A 15th century church and a high street lined with antiques shops make it a popular stop for tourists.

4 Lechlade

The highest navigable point on the River Thames, with a Halfpenny Bridge *(dating back to the 18th century)* that crosses it into the town centre. The true romance of the town is in the vicinity of St Lawrence church, where in 1815, the poet Shelley was inspired to write "Stanzas in a Summer Churchyard".

If you're brave enough, try emulating the students and explore Oxford by bike.

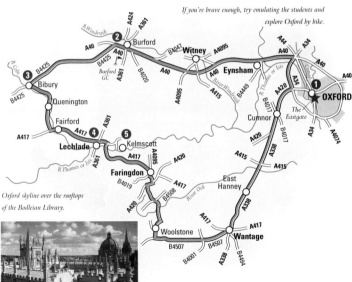

Oxford skyline over the rooftops of the Bodleian Library.

3 Bibury

A freshwater trout farm, which includes an extensive breeding programme, is one of the attractions of this small village on the fringe of the Cotswolds.

5 Kelmscott Manor

This Tudor home, near the town of Lechlade, was the summer residence of archetypal English designer William Morris, whose decor is preserved within the house.

Local attractions/events:
Open all year (except some public holidays) unless otherwise shown

Oxford:
(also refer to page 117)

Bodleian Library: a 15th century Divinity School, the 17th century Old Schools Quadrangle, an Exhibition Room and guided tours of Convocation House and Duke Humfrey's Library
Museum of the History of Science: optical, horological, mathematical and scientific instruments from medieval times to the present day
St Michael at the North Gate: a Saxon tower and viewpoint, it is Oxford's oldest building
University Church of St Mary the Virgin: also provides an alternative vantage point to look over Oxford's skyline
Pitt Rivers Museum: from toys to totem poles – an ethnological collection of exhibits in an historic Victorian setting
Rotunda Museum of Antique Dolls Houses: a private collection of over 40 historic dolls houses from 1700-1900 *(May-Sep, limited times)*
Inspector Morse Tours: follow in the footsteps of TV's celebrated detective, with lots of lively anecdotes along the way

Surrounding areas:
(also refer to pages 45 & 147)

Swalcliffe Barn, *Swalcliffe Lea:* built by New College Oxford between 1401-1409, it is one of England's finest barns, now housing some of the country's past agricultural and trade vehicles, as well as exhibitions of local archaeology and history *(Apr-Oct)*
Cotswold Wildlife Park, *Burford:* set in 160 acres of gardens and parkland around a Victorian manor house, it has numerous attractions to keep the whole family entertained *(Apr-Oct)*

Heritage Hotels – Oxford

The Randolph

Beaumont Street, Oxford OX1 2LN *See map page 4*
Tel: (0)870 400 8200 Fax: (0)186 579 2133 Regional General Manager: James Stewart
E-mail: HeritageHotels_Oxford.Randolph@forte-hotels.com
Reservations: (0)870 400 8855 www.heritage-hotels.com

How to get there:
Following signs to the city centre leads directly to St Giles. Prominent on the corner, to your right, you will spy the Randolph.

Facilities:
119 bedrooms, 9 suites, 7 mini-suites, 5 half-testers, 1 four-poster, 24-hour room service, hairdryer, trouser press, satellite TV, restaurant, bar and bistro, Chapters bar, open fires in winter, car park adjacent (special terms available for hotel guests).

Family:
Baby listening, baby sitting.

Leisure rates pppn

Midweek:	BB	DBB
Apr 2000	£ 85	£105
May–Nov	£ 99	£129
Dec–Mar 2001	£ 85	£105
Weekend:	BB	DBB
Apr 2000	£ 79	£ 99
May–Nov	£ 89	£109
Dec–Mar 2001	£ 85	£105

Luxury at the Randolph rates
Validity dates: all dates until March 2001 – subject to availability
May–November
£280 per person for two nights
December–April
£255 per person for two nights
Upgrade to suite
£40 per person for two nights
Based on two sharing.
Wine not included with meals
Please quote 'Special Break' when booking.

Chapters Bar and Fellows' Lounge are popular meeting places often featured on screen (Debra Winger and Anthony Hopkins were there for Shadowlands, and TV's *Inspector Morse* is a regular). Plush Victorian burgundy decor and opulent candlelit settings in the Spires Restaurant and conspire to make dining a sybaritic experience.

Luxury at the Randolph:
Right in the heart of the city, the Randolph has been home to royalty, elder statesmen and celebrities and is Oxford's premier hotel.

The hotel is within an easy walk of museums, shops and theatres. Waiting in your room on arrival will be champagne, flowers and chocolates.

Enjoy one of Ailish's champagne cocktails in the Chapters Bar, the setting for many Inspector Morse novels, then a 3-course meal in the Spires Restaurant with coffee and petits fours in Fellows' Lounge. Enjoy a leisurely breakfast the next day before having a tour of Oxford on the open-topped bus, which will pick you up from right outside the hotel. Entry tickets are arranged to nearby Blenheim Palace (15 minutes' drive), the home of the Duke of Marlborough (available only until the end of October – although the gardens designed by 'Capability' Brown are open throughout the year), followed by afternoon tea at the romantic Bear Hotel

at Woodstock. No doubt you will be ready for another of Ailish's cocktails after all this sightseeing, and again the Spires Restaurant is the setting for your evening meal. After breakfast, before you depart, as a memento of your stay in Oxford, you will be presented with an *Inspector Morse* novel signed by the author, Colin Dexter.

What's included in your break:
• 2 nights' dinner, bed and breakfast
• champagne, chocolates and flowers on the first night
• one of Ailish's champagne cocktails each evening before your meal
• a tour of Oxford on the first morning
• entry to Blenheim Palace
• afternoon tea at the Bear in Woodstock
• one copy per couple of a signed Inspector Morse novel

Oxford – Oxfordshire

1 Ashmolean Museum

Britain's oldest public museum was founded in 1683. Among its displays are diverse collections of British, European, Egyptian and Eastern antiquities; European paintings and sculpture; and Indian and Oriental art. Particularly popular are the coins and medals housed in the Heberden Coin Room.

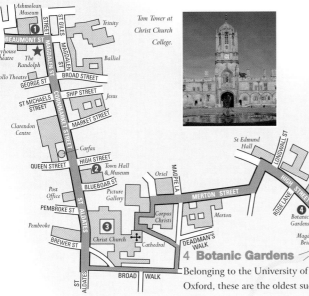

Tom Tower at Christ Church College.

2 Museum of Oxford

From prehistoric to modern times, Oxford's history is uncovered in this small museum. Six 'Oxford rooms' re-create city interiors through the ages, from an Elizabethan Inn to a Victorian kitchen.

Magdalen Bridge showing the River Cherwell and Botanic Garden.

3 Christ Church College

Founded in 1249, Oxford University, the oldest in Britain, comprises 36 colleges, and its 25,000 students are a central feature of the city. Christ Church college features a 16th century chapel that serves as the city's cathedral. Many of the other colleges have notable architectural features.

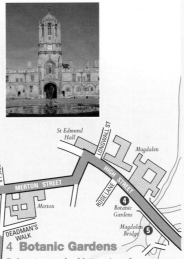

4 Botanic Gardens

Belonging to the University of Oxford, these are the oldest such gardens in the country. Created in the early 17th century, the walled gardens contain medicinal herbs as well as a diverse collection of international plants. Glasshouses contain a collection of lilies and palms.

5 Magdalen Bridge

One of the overriding images of the university city, and of England, is that of students *(and tourists)* punting down the river. Punts are flat-bottomed, shallow-water boats steered with long poles. They can be hired at various points along the river, but the Magdalen Bridge is one of the most popular and central.

Local attractions/events:

Open all year (except some public holidays) unless otherwise shown

Oxford:
(also refer to page 115)

Christ Church Picture Gallery: superb collections of paintings and drawings from the 14th-18th centuries

Museum of Natural History: a natural history collection set in a splendid Victorian gothic building

Carfax Tower: this 72ft high tower offers magnificent views over Oxford's famous skyline but beware – it has 99 steps to climb!

Bate Collection: historical woodwind, brass, percussion and keyboard instruments are on display from all over Europe

Museum of Modern Art: an acclaimed centre for the display of 20th century visual culture

Curioxity: a hands on science exhibition for all ages

Ghost Tours: take a walk on the darkside of Oxford's streets and alleyways in search of the city's ghoulish past *(Jul-Sep)*

University of Oxford Real Tennis Club: home of 'real' tennis for over 400 years

Oxford from the River: take one of the scheduled river cruises or hire a punt *(with chauffeur, if required)*, rowing or electric boats on the Cherwell or Thames *(Apr-Oct)*

Surrounding areas:
(also refer to pages 45 & 147)

Fairford: once an important stage on the London to Gloucester coaching run, the town contains numerous 17th and 18th century buildings, as well as St Mary's Church – a 15th century church with fine examples of medieval stained glass

Folly Farm Waterfowl Park, Bourton-on-the-Water: in 50 acres of Cotswold parkland, it is home to nearly 170 rare and distinctly differing breeds plus goats, llamas, rheas and highland cattle

Heritage Hotels – Padstow

The Metropole

Station Road, Padstow, Cornwall PL28 8DB *See map page 2*
Tel: (0)870 400 8122 Fax: (0)184 153 2867
General Manager: Hervé Goulet E-mail: HeritageHotels_Padstow.Metropole@forte-hotels.com
Reservations: (0)870 400 8855 www.heritage-hotels.com

How to get there:
Locate the B3890, off the A389 near Wadebridge, then follow this road down into the town, around Padstow docks, which are overlooked by the Metropole.

Facilities: 50 bedrooms, 3 four-posters (1 with balcony), 5 mini-suites (1 with balcony), restaurant, bar, lounge, heated outdoor pool (open July–August only), hairdryer, trouser press and free car park.

Padstow is a paradise for those who love seafood. Its views are pretty spectacular, too – particularly from the Metropole, an imposing Victorian hotel which stands on a hill overlooking the harbour and Camel estuary. Padstow's narrow streets are dotted with small colourful shops and you can find amazing antiques. Or walk along the beaches and find clams.

Leisure rates pppn

All Week	BB	DBB
Apr–Jun 2000	£ 64	£ 74
Jul–Sep	£ N/A	£ 84
Oct–Nov	£ 64	£ 74
Dec–Feb	£ 45	£ 59
March 2001	£ 64	£ 74

Special Break 1 rates
3-night (mid-week) break
May–October 2000
£230 per person

Special Break 2 rates
3-night (mid-week) break
November–February
£165 per person
Please quote 'Special Break' when booking.

Special Break 1:

Check into your sea view room and a welcome of champagne and chocolates. Enjoy a complimentary aperitif each evening prior to dinner. Tickets will be provided for you to visit The Lost Gardens of Heligan (May–October) at your leisure. Enjoy a light lunch or cream tea each day in the Sun Terrace overlooking the estuary.

What's included in your break:
• champagne and chocolates in your room on arrival
• 3 nights' accommodation
• English breakfast
• 3-course menu dinner (wine not included)
• aperitif each evening prior to dinner
• tickets to the Lost Gardens of Heligan
• light lunch or cream tea

Special Break 2:

Check into your sea view room, then relax in the lounge and enjoy a cream tea. A pre-dinner drink and a bottle of (house) wine with dinner each evening is also included. Enjoy a light lunch or cream tea on each of the other days, and a complimentary aperitif each evening prior to dinner. Tickets will be provided for you to visit the Lost Gardens of Heligan (May–October) at your leisure. Enjoy a late lunch or cream tea each day in the Sun Terrace overlooking the estuary.

What's included in your break:
• 3 nights' accommodation
• English breakfast
• 3-course menu dinner (one bottle of house wine per couple included)
• aperitif each evening prior to dinner
• cream tea (day 1)
• light lunch or cream tea (days 2 & 3)

Padstow – Cornwall

1 Prideaux Place

Tucked into the hillside above the town, it was built in 1592 by Sir Nicholas Prideaux. The Elizabethan façade remains instantly recognisable, although successive generations have embraced a wide variety of styles. It contains magnificent collections of porcelain, portraits, furniture and paintings and has undergone major restoration in the last ten years. *(Mar-Oct)*

2 Polzeath

Cornwall's thriving surfing industry is centred around Polzeath, with its high and ferocious waves. The beaches are regularly dotted with avid contenders, and tuition is offered for beginners.

4 Polperro

One of Cornwall's most picturesque villages, which has thrived on its fishing industry, is made all the more romantic with its history of 19th century smuggling.

The picturesque Polperro harbour and town.

The ruined castle of Tintagel is popularly considered to be the birthplace of the legendary King Arthur.

3 Tintagel

Popularly considered to be the birthplace of King Arthur, the ruined castle of this Cornish village was eventually destroyed by the elements, despite early attempts to rebuild it. Ruins of an old Celtic monastery are also nearby.

5 St Austell

St Austell is known largely for its production of porcelain china, made out of local clay, which was once thought to exist only in the Far East. The industry has thrived since the 18th century.

Local attractions/events:

Open all year (except some public holidays) unless otherwise shown

Surrounding areas:

Rumps Cliff Castle, *Polzeath:* a beautiful promontory fortification, which consists of four defensive ramparts, only two of which were in use at any one time

Pencarrow House, *Washaway:* award-winning Georgian country house with superb paintings, porcelain and furniture. Internationally renowned Grade II listed gardens *(Mar-Oct)*

Military Museum, *Bodmin:* one of the best of its kind, it has fascinating displays of small arms, medals, badges, uniforms, pictures and much more!

Bodmin & Wexford Railway: branch line steam railway along the River Fowey Valley and Boscarne, on the Camel Trail *(Mar-Oct)*

St Petroc's Church, *Bodmin:* 15th century church with a Norman fort, the largest parish church in Cornwall *(Mar-Sep, limited times)*

Lanhydrock, *Bodmin:* the grandest and most welcoming house in Cornwall, it dates from 1651 but was largely rebuilt after a fire in 1881. 50 rooms give an extraordinary glimpse into Victorian life. Set in 450 acres of gardens and woodland *(Mar-Oct)*

Restormel Castle, *Lostwithiel:* perched on a high mound, surrounded by a dry moat, the huge circular keep of this splendid castle survives in remarkably good condition *(Apr-Oct)*

Museum, *Lostwithiel:* housed in the old town prison, it has an excellent collection of photographs *(Mar-Sep)*

St Catherine's Castle, *Fowey:* a small gun fort built by Henry VIII to defend Fowey harbour

Lanreath Folk and Farm Museum, *Nr Looe:* a hands-on experience for all age groups *(Mar-Oct)*

Heritage Hotels – Romsey

The White Horse

Market Place, Romsey, Hampshire SO51 8ZJ *See map page 4*
Tel: (0)870 400 8123 Fax: (0)179 451 7485 General Manager: Anne Hutchinson
E-mail: HeritageHotels_Romsey.White_Horse@forte-hotels.com
Reservations: (0)870 400 8855 www.heritage-hotels.com

How to get there:

After leaving the M27 at junction 3, follow the A3057 to Romsey, then follow signs to the town centre and Market Place. Drive past the hotel and take the first turning left into Latimer Street, which will deliver you into the hotel car park.

Facilities: 33 bedrooms, hairdryer, trouser press, restaurant, bar, lounges, free swimming pool and fitness centre nearby, free car park.

Family: Baby listening, baby sitting

The Regency façade conceals a building that dates in part back to the 14th century. The hotel is a short walk from Broadlands, the 18th-century house where Lord Palmerston, Queen Victoria's Prime Minister, and Lord Mountbatten once lived. A series of Tudor wall paintings has recently been unearthed at the hotel, oak beams are in abundance, and traces exist of an Elizabethan mummers' gallery. An old courtyard dating back to its coaching inn days is a popular stop for drinks.

Leisure rates pppn

All Week	BB	DBB
Apr 2000	£ 38	£ 54
May–Nov	£ 42	£ 60
Dec–Mar 2001	£ 38	£ 54

Special Break rates

Validity date:
July and August 2000
November 2000–March 2001
Leisure rates
Please quote 'Special Break' when booking.

Special Break:

Enjoy a complimentary visit to Broadlands, the home of Lord and Lady Romsey. This superb Palladian mid- Georgian house is about 10 minutes' walk from the hotel and a truly lovely stately home with landscaped gardens by 'Capability' Brown. Previous occupants of Broadlands have included Lord Palmerston and Lord Mountbatten.

What's included in your break:
• visit to Broadlands.

Special Break: (From November onwards)

A free visit to the famous National Motor Museum at Beaulieu in the heart of the New Forest has been arranged. The museum is well known for its collection of cars and motorcycles but is also next door to the Palace House and gardens, which form part of the visit.

What's included in your break:
• ticket entrance to the National Motor Museum at Beaulieu
• ticket entrance to the Palace House and its gardens

Romsey – Hampshire

1 Romsey Abbey

Romsey Abbey was the site of a Benedictine nunnery in Norman times, and the grand architecture of the church is a mark of the respect the order gained from the community. Oak trees from the New Forest were used for the roof timbers. In the 16th century, the people of Romsey bought the church from the king, and it has since been Romsey's parish church.

4 Lyndhurst

The central town of the New Forest, where you will find information about trails and walks in the area. The town is also the burial site of Alice Liddel, who as a little girl inspired Lewis Carroll's stories of Alice in Wonderland.

Typical thatched cottage at Lyndhurst.

Beaulieu palace and garden.

2 Broadlands

The birthplace of Lord Palmerston, the mid-19th century prime minister, Broadlands was also the home of Lord Louis Mountbatten. The Prince and Princess of Wales spent part of their honeymoon in the Georgian house. *(Apr-Sep)*

3 Rufus Stone

In the heart of the New Forest is this monument to King William II *(also known as William Rufus)*, assassinated here in 1100. The murderer is unknown, but the prime suspect was William's brother, who ascended the throne as King Henry I.

5 Beaulieu

This stately home, standing on the site of a former abbey, is best known for its National Motor Museum, a collection of 250 motor vehicles, ranging from classic cars from the early days of motoring, through to the land-speed racer, the Bluebird. An exhibition also explains the history of automobiles.

Local attractions/events:
Open all year (except some public holidays) unless otherwise shown

Surrounding areas:

Mottisfont Abbey, *nr Romsey:* a 12th century Augustinian priory but now a house of some note, with delightful rooms such as the drawing room, decorated by Rex Whistler. The grounds feature an enchanting riverside walk *(Mar-Oct)*

Sir Harold Hillier Gardens & Arboretum, *Ampfield:* rare and beautiful plants from around the world, set in 180 acres – literally 'a garden for all seasons' providing interest and colour all year round

Paultons Park, *Ower:* a great family day out with rides, attractions, dinosaurs and exotic birds *(Mar-Oct, Nov-Dec weekends only)*

Eling Tide Mill, *Totton:* natural tide power harnessed in the only surviving tide mill still producing wholemeal flour in a centuries-old tradition

Totton & Eling Heritage Centre: the history of this area from the Stone Age until WWII. Tableaux, panels and artefacts, including a 3,000 year old dagger

Breamore House and Museum, *nr Fordingbridge:* an Elizabethan manor house set in a Tudor village, where visitors are taken back to when the community was self-sufficient *(Apr-Sep)*

Rockbourne Roman Villa, *nr Fordingbridge:* remains of the largest known Roman villa in the region – discover what life would have been like in Roman Britain over 1600 years ago *(Apr-Sep)*

Exbury Gardens, *nr Beaulieu:* with its world famous displays of rhododendrons and azaleas, the 200 acre grounds also offer 'special events' during the year

Bucklers Hard, *nr Beaulieu:* 18th century village with historic cottage displays and a Maritime Museum. Alternatively, enjoy a cruise on the Beaulieu River *(Apr-Oct)*

St Margaret's Church, *3 miles west of Romsey:* this is the burial place of Florence Nightingale

Heritage Hotels – St Andrews

Rusacks

Plimour Links, St Andrews, Fife KY16 9JQ *See map page 13*
Tel: (0)870 400 8128 Fax: (0)133 447 7896 Regional General Manager: Joe Longmuir
E-mail: HeritageHotels_StAndrews.Rusacks@forte-hotels.com
Reservations: (0)870 400 8855 www.heritage-hotels.com

How to get there:
Rusacks Hotel sits adjacent to the coastal A91, with junction 8 of the M90 26 miles away.

Facilities: 44 bedrooms,
4 suites, many rooms overlooking the golf course and St Andrews Bay, 24-hour room service, hairdryer, trouser press, satellite TV, golf club, bar, log fires in winter, free car park. Sauna and solarium.

Family: Baby listening

Leisure rates pppn

	BB	DBB
Apr 2000	£ 55	£ 70
May–Jun	£ 85	£105
Jul–Aug	£105	£125
Sep–Oct	£ 95	£115
Nov–Mar 2001	£ 55	£ 70

Special Break rates
£60 per person supplement to the Leisure Break Rate
Validity dates:
until 31–March 2001
(Excludes 23–29 April, 22–26 June, 17–24 July, 10–15 October, 18–19 October, 23–24 October, 23–27 December 2000, 30 December–2 January 2001)

Please quote 'Special Break' when booking.

Guests who have stayed at Rusacks include golfing and rock and roll legends. Originally opened in 1887, it has been stylishly remodelled on a golfing theme to take advantage of its prestigious location and eye-catching views over the 18th green of the Old Course.

The Old Course Bar and Restaurant, which has a dramatic view of the famous course, specialises in seafood and game dishes.

Rusacks has an in-house golf club with a resident golf manager, changing rooms, a sauna solarium, pro-shop and bar.

Special Break:
Turn your Forte Leisure Break into the perfect golfer's indulgence: take tips from one of St Andrews PGA Professionals with a golf lesson captured on video for posterity. Back in the comfort of your home, what better way to remember your relaxing break than re-living your lesson accompanied by a dram of whisky from your new engraved decanter and glasses? This special gift from the hotel depicts St Andrews and the Swilken Bridge, the ideal souvenir of a trip to the Home of Golf.

St Andrews – Fife

1 St Andrews

The centre of life in St Andrews is its university, the oldest in Scotland, and tours of the 15th-century buildings are possible. The cathedral is also an important historic site. It dates from the 12th century but fell into ruin during the Reformation.

3 Anstruther

The main industry of this small town is fishing, and a museum dedicated to the industry makes a fascinating visit. An old fisherman's cottage and a boatyard are part of the display.

4 Crail

One of the most attractive of the fishing villages along this coast also benefits from a beach and a golf course. A taste of the seafood that gives the village its livelihood is recommended in one of the restaurants.

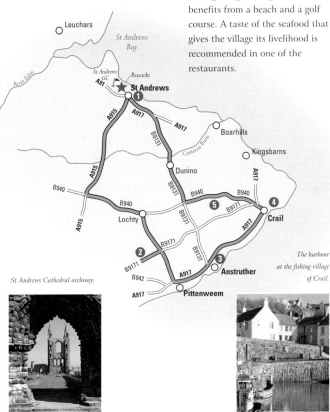

St Andrews Cathedral archway.

The harbour at the fishing village of Crail.

2 Kellie Castle & Gardens

A fine example of Lowland Scottish domestic architecture, dating from 1360. Restored in the 19th century, it has many varied and interesting attractions including a Victorian nursery and an old kitchen. *(Mar-Oct)*

5 Scottish Bunker

A simple farmhouse is the 'undercover' entrance of this bunker. Set up during the Cold War for government use in case of nuclear attack, in 1994 it was opened to the public as a museum dedicated to the 1950s era of nuclear obsession.

Local attractions/events:

Open all year (except some public holidays) unless otherwise shown

St Andrews:

Castle & Visitors' Centre: rare examples of medieval siege techniques and the bottle dungeon hollowed out of solid rock from which death was the only escape

Cathedral: the remains still give a vivid impression of the scale of what was once the largest cathedral in Scotland. Climb St Roles Tower for a magnificent view of the area

Museum: it recounts the heritage of this unique city from medieval to modern times

Royal & Ancient Golf Club: dating from the 1750's, the Old Course is the venue for the British Open, and the Museum of British Golf here traces its origins up to the personalities of today

Craigtown Country Park: in beautiful surroundings, it offers a wide range of facilities for all the family

Sea Life Centre: the chance to see hundreds of sea creatures, many of which are native to Scottish waters

Surrounding areas:

Folkland Palace, *Cupar:* country residence of 8 Stuart monarchs, including Mary Queen of Scots, built in 1597 *(Apr-Oct)*

Hill of Tarvit Mansionhouse & Garden, *Ceres:* a fine country house with a notable collection of furniture, paintings, porcelain and bronzes

St Monan's Windmill: this windmill tower is the only upstanding remnant of a wider industrial complex dating from the 18th century *(Jun-Aug)*

Museum & Heritage Centre, *Crail:* it provides an insight into the seafaring traditions of this ancient Royal Burgh *(May-Sep)*

Pottery Centre, *Crail:* a working pottery in beautifully restored medieval buildings

Heritage Hotels – Salisbury

The White Hart

St John Street, Salisbury, Wiltshire SP1 2SD *See map page 4*
Tel: (0)870 400 8125 Fax: (0)1722 412 761 General Manager: Peter Watt
E-mail: HeritageHotels_Salisbury.White_Hart@forte-hotels.com
Reservations: (0)870 400 8855 www.heritage-hotels.com

How to get there:

Follow the ring road to its southernmost point and then turn into Exeter Street, towards the city centre. The hotel is on the right-hand side.

Facilities: 68 bedrooms, 3 four-posters, restaurant, lounge and bar, open fires in winter, free car park at rear.

Family: Baby listening, baby sitting on request.

Leisure rates pppn

Midweek:	BB	DBB
Apr 2000	£ 70	£ 85
May–Jun	£ 75	£ 90
Jul–Aug	£ 58	£ 73
Sep–Nov	£ 70	£ 85
Dec–Feb	£ 58	£ 73
March 2001	£ 60	£ 75
Weekend:	BB	DBB
Apr 2000	£ 60	£ 75
May–Jun	£ 65	£ 80
Jul–Aug	£ 58	£ 73
Sep–Nov	£ 65	£ 80
Dec–Feb	£ 55	£ 70
March 2001	£ 58	£ 73

A White Hart Connoisseur Break rates

2-night programme
£185 per person
(April–October), £170
(November–March)
*Please quote 'Special Break'
when booking.*

A Georgian landmark with sweeping facade and pillared portico, the architecture of the White Hart has undergone some sympathetic 20th-century restoration. Try the luxury of the St Catherine suite with its balcony over the portico, one of the three rooms with glorious four-posters. In winter, huge log fires burn in open fireplaces, and in summer months the courtyard is a tapestry of colour with flower displays. Salisbury is ringed by prehistoric forts and mystic stone circles, the most famous one being Stonehenge.

A White Hart Connoisseur Break:

Arrive on Friday night to a warm welcome. In the bedroom you will find a welcome gift of chilled champagne, fudge and a complimentary guidebook to the city. Savour a candlelit dinner in the restaurant from the full à la carte menu followed by a complimentary liqueur or cognac with your coffee in the delightful lounge or courtyard. After a relaxing night's sleep, explore the city on the guided walk from the Guild Hall and then in the afternoon take in the magnificent cathedral with the tallest spire in Britain. Return to the hotel for a traditional cream tea. On Saturday evening enjoy another fine dinner in the restaurant and after a comfortable night, depart after breakfast on Sunday via Winchester and the Wessex Hotel to enjoy a traditional Sunday lunch and tour this fascinating city.

What's included in your break:
• 2 nights' dinner, bed and breakfast
• a welcome gift of champagne and fudge
• a guidebook to the city of Salisbury
• 3-course dinner from the full à la carte menu *(wine not included)*
• complimentary liqueur or cognac with your coffee
• full English breakfast both days
• full traditional tea *(Saturday)*
• traditional Sunday lunch at the Wessex Heritage Hotel *(Winchester)*

Salisbury – Wiltshire

1 Salisbury Cathedral

13th century cathedral with the tallest spire in England, reaching 404 feet. The interior is notable for its natural light, and its library, which contains an original copy of the Magna Carta.

2 Wilton House

Elizabethan house designed by the great architect Inigo Jones and one of the finest stately homes in England. It is worth a visit for its art collection, and illustrations of scenes from *Arcadia*, written by the 16th century poet Sir Philip Sidney while he was living at Wilton.

4 Stourhead

The main attraction of this stately home is its beautiful, landscaped gardens, reminiscent of Renaissance Italy. The owner commissioned the design in the 1750s, filling the grounds with lakes, bridges and statues, among other features.

5 Old Sarum Castle

The massive Iron Age hillfort of old Sarum *(Old Salisbury)* was reused by the Romans, Saxons and Normans before becoming a flourishing medieval settlement. This dramatic site contains the ruins of a castle, cathedral and Bishop's palace and provide fine views of the surrounding countryside. Special events take place in the summer.

Stained glass window at Salisbury Cathedral.

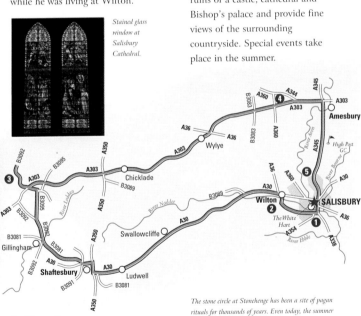

The stone circle at Stonehenge has been a site of pagan rituals for thousands of years. Even today, the summer solstice is celebrated in the area.

3 Stonehenge

One of Britain's most famous and precious sites, a UNESCO World Heritage Site, this prehistoric stone circle still baffles historians. Dating as far back as 3000BC, we still do not know how these massive stones were transported here, but the mystery adds to the attraction.

Local attractions/events:
Open all year (except some public holidays) unless otherwise shown

Salisbury:

Salisbury and South Wiltshire Museum: set in a 17th century, Grade 1 listed building, it is designated as having archaeological collections of national importance

The Wardrobe: dating from 1254, it takes its name from being used as a clothing and document store by bishops in the 14th century. It now serves as a museum with exhibits telling an absorbing story of English county regiments

Mompesson House: a perfect example of Queen Anne architecture, built in 1701. It contains the important Turnbull collection of 18th century drinking glasses, fine period furniture, an elegantly carved oak staircase and a charming walled garden *(Apr-Oct)*

The Medieval Hall: a 40 minute introduction to this colourful city, you can discover the secrets of Salisbury in a sound and picture presentation *(Apr-Sep)*

Racecourse: racing has taken place here since the 16th century and today it stages evening meetings as well *(May-Sep)*

Larmer Tree Gardens: created in 1880, it is inhabited by pheasants, peacocks and macaws *(Apr-Oct)*

Surrounding areas:
(also refer to pages 109, 121 & 141)

The Carpet Factory, *Wilton:* in the 18th century courtyard, this exhibition unravels the mysteries of carpet making by the world famous names of *Wilton* and *Axminster,* spanning 300 years. Demonstrations of manufacture by traditional methods using powerlooms

A Music at Leisure Weekend hotel – see pages 32-33
A Murder Mystery Weekend hotel – see pages 34-37

127

Heritage Hotels – Staines

The Thames Lodge

Thames Street, Staines, Middlesex TW18 4SE *See map page 4*
Tel: (0)870 400 8121 Fax: (0)178 445 4858 General Manager: Michael Stout
E-mail: HeritageHotels_Staines.Thames_Lodge@forte-hotels.com
Reservations: (0)870 400 8855 www.heritage-hotels.com

How to get there:

Leave the M25 at junction 13 and join the A30 to London. At Crooked Billet roundabout, follow signs for Staines town centre. Continue on this road and the hotel is directly in front of you at the T-junction. The car park is to the right of the hotel.

Facilities: 79 bedrooms,
hairdryer, trouser press, brasserie and terrace overlooking the Thames, bar, lounge, function suites, Thames Lodge Conference Centre *(converted cottages with direct access to the hotel's riverside terrace).*

Leisure rates pppn

Midweek:	BB	DBB
Apr 2000	£ 85	£100
May–Nov	£ 90	£105
Dec–Mar 2001	£ 85	£100
Weekend:	BB	DBB
Apr–Mar 2001	£ 45	£ 60

Special Break rates

Validity dates:
20 March 2000 – 20 March 2001
£125 per person
(based on two people sharing)
Single supplement
£10 per person per night
Please quote 'Special Break'
when booking.

A rambling, mainly 19th-century building with a modern extension sitting right on the banks of the river, the hotel still has its own moorings, a tradition dating back to the days when it was known as the Packhorse and was used as a stopping spot for barges being hauled up the river by horses. Visitors enjoy the sights of the river from the lounge and the Brasserie Restaurant, and those who have plumped for a bedroom on the top floor have an almost panoramic view – a pleasant surprise in a hotel which is only 19 miles from central London.

Special Break:

Day 1 – Arrive at your leisure, check in to one of the recently refurbished rooms, and enjoy dinner in the Brasserie Restaurant overlooking the River Thames.

Day 2 – After breakfast, you are invited to visit Hampton Court with the hotel's compliments. This is England's finest royal palace, with over 500 years of history, and is situated on the banks of the River Thames. Follow in the footsteps of some of the greatest kings and queens through the magnificent state apartments, Great Hall and Chapel Royal. In the afternoon, a visit to Windsor Castle is recommended. Return to the hotel to relax with an aperitif in the lounge and reflect over dinner on the wonders of the day.

Day 3 – After a hearty English breakfast, check out of the hotel, and before you leave for home, we recommend either a walk along the River Thames at Eton, or a visit to the beautiful Savill Garden.

What's included in your break:
• 2 nights' dinner, bed and breakfast
• ticket to Hampton Court
  (opens every day except 24th–26th December.
  Mid-March to mid-October 9.30am to 6pm.
  Last admission 45 minutes before closing)
• 3-course table d'hôte dinner menu
  (coffee included)

Staines – Middlesex

1 Runnymede

On 15 June 1215, King John signed the Magna Carta at Runnymede, a document that not only prevented civil war in his reign, but laid down the foundations of a justice system that exists today throughout the civilised world. A memorial marks the site of this historic event.

2 Royal Holloway College

Modelled on a French château, the grand building, which now houses part of the University of London, was constructed in the 1880s for Thomas Holloway as a women's college. Turrets and gables help to conjure up the intended castle imagery. Inside the main college building is a fine collection of Victorian art.

4 Thorpe Park

The theme of this park is largely on water, such as the Thunder River white water ride. It is particularly popular with children, who enjoy the soaking that is the result of almost every ride. *(Apr-Oct)*

The Thunder River Ride is the most popular attraction at Thorpe Park.

5 Kempton Racecourse

Often dubbed 'London's racecourse', it is the nearest racing circuit to the capital, making it a popular day-trip for avid race-goers, especially for the season's premier fixture, The Pertemps Christmas Festival. A statue of the award-winning horse Desert Orchid overlooks the Parade ground.

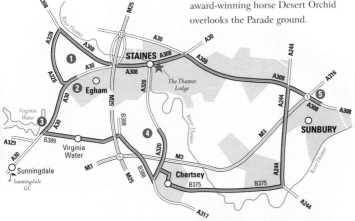

Local attractions/events:

Open all year (except some public holidays) unless otherwise shown

Staines:

Within a short driving distance from London's main airport (Heathrow), it is ideally situated as a communication link into the capital and all of its attractions, as well as the surrounding areas of Ascot, Kingston and Windsor

Surrounding areas:

(also refer to pages 51, 97 & 145)

Pleasure Grounds:
opposite the Runnymede Meadows is this relaxing riverside park, giving access to walks along the River, including the Thames Path National Trail and local countryside

Kempton Park Racecourse hosts 22 days of quality racing throughout the year.

Virginia Water:
this Surrey village was also the subject of Thomas Holloway's vision as a site for his sanitorium. Rumour has it that there is a secret underground passage between the college and the sanatorium, but this has never been proved
Chertsey Museum,
Chertsey: Displays tell the story of the Runnymede area and Chertsey Abbey. With a fine costume collection and a 'discovery room', temporary exhibitions are organised throughout the year
Abbeyfields, Chertsey: once the site of the Abbey, it is now a park
Thames Boats: relax on a 45 minute scenic trip from Walton Bridge via Shepperton *(Apr-Sep)*

3 Virginia Water Lake

Said to be named after Queen Elizabeth I *(the Virgin Queen)* within the grounds stands a one hundred foot totem pole weighing twelve tons. On the northern banks is Smiths Lawn, home of the Guards Polo Club.

Late afternoon at Virginia Water, in the snow.

Heritage Hotels – Stratford-upon-Avon

The Alveston Manor

Clopton Bridge, Stratford-upon-Avon, Warwickshire CV37 7HP *See map page 4*
Tel: (0)870 400 8181 Fax: (0)178 941 4095 Regional General Manager: Jim Souter
E-mail: HeritageHotels_Stratford_upon_Avon.Alveston_Manor@forte-hotels.com
Reservations: (0)870 400 8855 www.heritage-hotels.com

How to get there:
Leave the M40 at junction 15, taking the A46 and the A439 towards Stratford. Join the

one-way system, and keeping left towards Banbury and Oxford you'll find The Alveston Manor just over the bridge at the junction of the A422 and A3400.

Facilities: 114 bedrooms, 6 suites, room service, hairdryer, trouser press, satellite TV, Manor Grill *(AA Rosette)*, terrace/bar, free car park.

Family: Baby listening

Leisure rates pppn

Midweek:	BB	DBB
Apr–Jun 2000	£ 84	£ 99
Jul–Aug	£ 70	£ 80
Sep–Nov	£ 89	£ 99
Dec–Mar 2001	£ 84	£ 94
Weekend:	BB	DBB
Apr–Jun 2000	£ 74	£ 89
Jul–Aug	£ 70	£ 80
Sep–Mar 2001	£ 77	£ 87

Shakespeare's Stratford rates

This special theatre weekend is £200 per person for two nights, based on two people sharing a standard twin or double room. Supplements apply for upgrade to suites and executive accommodation. Weekends only from April 2000–end June 2000, plus any 2 nights between 21 July–30 August 2000 *Please quote 'Special Break' when booking.*

This is one of the finest bases from which to explore Stratford and surrounding areas. Rumour has it that the first performance of *A Midsummer's Night Dream* was given under the cedar tree that stands in the hotel's grounds. Leaded windows and an oak-panelled bar are mellow features of this hotel, as is the silver carving trolley in the award-winning Manor Grill.

Shakespeare's Stratford at the Alveston Manor:

The home of the Bard offers you a superb two-night theatre break at the Alveston Manor, where history is blended with modernity, creating a relaxing and comfortable location in the heart of England. Set on the south side of the River Avon, a five-minute walk across the ancient bridge will take you to interesting shops, the world-renowned theatre and the famous Shakespeare properties. The river bank is alive with narrow boats and wild fowl, the water meadows ideal for a leisurely walk on a beautiful evening, whatever the season. On arrival on Friday, you will find a bottle of champagne in your room, with flowers, chocolates and bathrobes. Dinner on your first night will be in the Manor Grill, with a pre-dinner Pimm's awaiting you in the cocktail bar. After breakfast on Saturday, tickets for the superb Guide Friday tour of Stratford in an open-topped bus will be available. While you are out and about, lunch in Othello's Bistro in the centre of town *(included in your package)* will fortify you for the

afternoon's sightseeing. Before departing for the theatre, your starter and main course will be served in the Manor Grill, with post-theatre dessert and liqueur at the hotel on your return. The Royal Shakespeare Theatre offers critically acclaimed productions throughout the year and no visit to Stratford-upon-Avon would be complete without this experience. After breakfast, before you depart, a copy of last night's play will be presented to you as a memento of your stay.

What's included in your break:
• 2 nights' dinner, bed and breakfast
• champagne, chocolates and flowers on arrival
• pre-dinner glass of Pimm's on Friday night
• tickets for Guide Friday tour of Stratford-upon-Avon on Saturday
• lunch in Othello's Bistro on Saturday
• two tickets for Saturday evening performance at the Royal Shakespeare Theatre
• one copy per couple of the play enjoyed
• complimentary copy of the performance programme

Stratford-upon-Avon – Warwickshire

1 Mary Arden's House and The Shakespeare Countryside Museum

The timbered farmhouse was the home of Shakespeare's mother before she married and moved to Stratford. It features many outbuilding displays about life and work on the land, with working blacksmiths, falconers, live stock and Glebe Farm.

2 Coughton Court

Home of the Throckmorton family since 1409, it has one of the finest collections of family portraits and memorabilia, a fine Tudor gatehouse, a half-timbered courtyard, walled gardens, a lake and riverside walks. *(Mar-Oct)*

3 Ragley Hall

Designed in 1680 by Robert Hooke in the Palladian style, emulating the Venetian architect Andrea Palladio. Inside is a priceless collection of furniture and art. *(Apr-Oct)*

4 Hidcote Manor Gardens

Internationally renowned, this is one of England's most beautiful and memorable gardens, which in reality is a series of special atmospheres. *(Apr-Nov)*

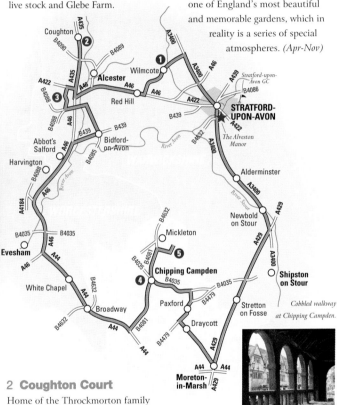

Cobbled walkway at Chipping Campden.

5 Chipping Campden

An authentic medieval town, and one of the most attractive in the area, Chipping Campden thrived on the wool industry. Today it buzzes again during the Cotswolds Games, a festival of bizarre but amusing country games.

Local attractions/events:

Open all year (except some public holidays) unless otherwise shown

Stratford-upon-Avon:
(also refer to pages 133 & 135)

Avon Cruises: boating on the river is an enjoyable pastime and, if you don't want to hire a punt or boat, regular passenger cruises are available in Edwardian craft or an 1898 Steam Launch *(Mar-Oct)*

Harvard House: the most ornate house in Stratford, a fine example of an Elizabethan house. Rebuilt in 1596, it was home to the mother of John Harvard, founder of the famous University. Contains the Neish collection of pewter *(Apr-Oct)*

Surrounding areas:
(also refer to page 53)

Racecourse: National Hunt racing with 14 fixtures in the season

Country villages & towns: providing easy access to the Cotswolds with pretty villages like Moreton-in-Marsh and Broadway, there are many other places to visit, such as Shipston-on-Stour with its elegant Georgian buildings, traditional coaching inns and 15th century parish church. Similarly, the two market towns of Alcester and Henley-in-Arden retain much of their historic charm, although the latter is possibly more famous today for its ice-cream

Chastleton House, Moreton-in-Marsh: one of the most complete Jacobean houses in England, it is filled with a mixture of rare and everyday objects, furniture and textiles – collected by generations of the same family since its completion in 1612

A Music at Leisure Weekend hotel – see pages 32-33
A Murder Mystery Weekend hotel – see pages 34-37

131

Heritage Hotels – Stratford-upon-Avon

The Shakespeare

Chapel Street, Stratford-upon-Avon, Warwickshire CV37 6ER *See map page 4*
Tel: (0)870 400 8182 Fax: (0)178 941 5411 Regional General Manager: Jim Souter
E-mail: HeritageHotels_Stratford_upon_Avon.Shakespeare@forte-hotels.com
Reservations: (0)870 400 8855 www.heritage-hotels.com

How to get there:
Leave the M40 at junction 15,
taking the A46 and the A439
towards Stratford. Join the
one-way system, take Bridge
Street to the roundabout
and then left into the
High Street, which leads
into Chapel Street.

Facilities: 70 bedrooms,
3 four-posters, 1 suite,
hairdryer, trouser press,
David Garrick Restaurant
(AA Rosette), bistro,
cocktail bar, lounge, open fire
in winter, free parking *(limited)*.
Family: Baby listening,
baby sitting.

Leisure rates pppn

Midweek:	BB	DBB
Apr–Jun 2000	£ 90	£105
Jul–Aug	£ 87	£102
Sep–Nov	£ 90	£105
Dec–Mar 2001	£ 87	£102
Weekend:	BB	DBB
Apr 2000	£ 89	£ 99
May–Nov	£ 92	£102
Dec–Feb 2001	£ 89	£ 99
Mar	£ 92	£102

The old stone floor remains in the reception area of this black and white Tudor-fronted hotel. Prince Charles has been here, as has Margaret Thatcher. In fact, the hotel's guest list has included many renowned names, particularly politicians, foreign diplomats and dedicated scholars pursuing the life and works of Shakespeare (including Elizabeth Taylor while engaged in *The Taming of the Shrew*, filmed with Richard Burton). Fittingly, each guest room has a connection with his plays. The Othello Restaurant has a traditional menu and an award-winning chef.

Visit the Stratford-upon-Avon Theatre, or Cox's Yard, an interactive centre, Charlecote Park *(where legend has it Shakespeare was caught poaching by the owner)*, and Warwick Castle.

Stratford-upon-Avon – Warwickshire

1 Shakespeare's Birthplace

Although it has never actually been proved that the great playwright was born here, these two-houses-in-one are treated as genuine. The interior is furnished as a 16th century home, emulating how Shakespeare may have lived, as well as displaying many items that belonged to him.

2 Royal Shakespeare Theatre

As its name suggests, the programme of performances here centres almost entirely on the many plays of Shakespeare. Backstage tours of the costumes and props departments are available.

The Royal Shakespeare Theatre, at night.

3 Holy Trinity Church

In a town obsessed with its past resident, the main claim to fame of this church is the burial tomb of Shakespeare himself. But moving away from the crowds, it is possible to appreciate the fine Gothic structure, which predates its well-known occupant.

4 Halls Croft

Shakespeare's daughter Susanna married the doctor John Hall and lived with him in this house. Today it houses an often unnerving museum dedicated to Elizabethan medicine.

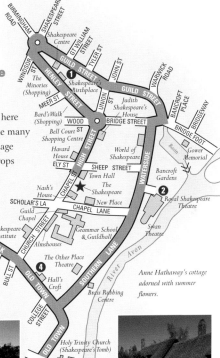

Anne Hathaway's cottage adorned with summer flowers.

5 Anne Hathaway's Cottage

This small thatched cottage was the early home of Anne Hathaway, who would become Shakespeare's wife. Original 16th century furniture is crammed into its tiny rooms. A Shakespeare garden features plants mentioned in the Bard's plays.

Local attractions/events:

Open all year (except some public holidays) unless otherwise shown

Stratford-upon-Avon:
(also refer to pages 131 & 135)

Shire Horse Centre: experience the largest horses in the world and learn how they worked in years gone by and their development from medieval warhorses *(Mar-Oct)*
International Flute Festival: world class concerts including classical, jazz and brass bands *(13-22 Oct)*
Nash's House and New Place: once owned by Thomas Nash, who married Shakespeare's grand-daughter, it contains exceptional furnishings of the time and displays on the history of Stratford *(Mar-Oct)*
Brass Rubbing Centre: make or buy beautiful brass rubbings to take home
Butterfly Farm: hundreds of spectacular and colourful butterflies, flying among exotic blossoms, splashing waterfalls and fish-filled pools *(summer)*
Country Artists Visitor Centre: tour the studios to experience the immense skills of artists painting figurines by hand
Teddy Bear Museum: hundreds of enchanting teddy bears displayed in a 'listed' Elizabethan building
Cox's Yard: home of the 'Stratford Tales' – a time travel journey to meet characters, hear legends and witness events through the centuries

Surrounding areas:

Snowhills Manor, *Mickleton:* Tudor House with a c.1700 façade, best known for Charles Paget Wade's collection of musical instruments, clocks, toys, bicycles, weavers tools and Samurai armour *(Apr-Oct)*
Heritage Motor Centre, *Gaydon:* the largest collection of British cars in the world *(Apr-Oct)*
The Saxon Sanctury, *Wootton Wawen:* St Peter's Church is Warwickshire's oldest and houses a colourful Arden heritage exhibition

Heritage Hotels – Stratford-upon-Avon

The Swan's Nest

Bridgefoot, Stratford-upon-Avon, Warwickshire CV37 7LT *See map page 4*
Tel: (0)870 400 8183 Fax: (0)178 941 4547 Regional General Manager: Jim Souter
E-mail: HeritageHotels_Stratford_upon_Avon.Swans_Nest@forte-hotels.com
Reservations: (0)870 400 8855 www.heritage-hotels.com

How to get there:
Leave the M40 at junction 15, taking the A46 for 2 miles. First island turn left onto A439 towards Stratford. Follow one-way system, turn left (A3400), over the bridge, the Swan's Nest is on the right.

Facilities: 68 bedrooms, restaurant, bar, lounge, free parking.
Family: Baby listening.

Leisure rates pppn

Midweek:	BB	DBB
Apr–Aug 2000	£ 56	£ 74
Sep–Dec	£ 66	£ 81
Jan–Mar 2001	£ 66	£ 81
Weekend:	**BB**	**DBB**
Apr–Aug 2000	£ 54	£ 69
Sep–Dec	£ 64	£ 79
Jan–Mar 2001	£ 64	£ 79

This hotel dates from the late 17th century and is one of the earliest brick houses built in the Stratford area. With its own river frontage, it is perfectly situated for an afternoon boating trip, or a leisurely stroll along the banks of the Avon before heading for the theatre, just a five-minute walk away. There is the River Bar, the informal Cygnet Restaurant with pre-theatre dinners and, after an unusually long performance, 24-hour room service.

Stratford-upon-Avon – Warwickshire

1 Charlecote Park

The Lucy family have occupied this site since 1247, and the park's mansion includes many memorials to past ancestors. The gardens, which include a croquet lawn accessible for public use, are still inhabited by roaming deer.

The mansion at Charlecote Park.

3 Kenilworth Castle

Home to John of Gaunt and Henry IV, this 12th century castle became the home of the popular Earl of Leicester in the 16th century. The Civil War left it in ruins, but it remains an impressive nod to history.

Jephson Gardens at Leamington Spa

Re-creation of a battle scene at Kenilworth Castle.

2 Warwick Castle

One of the most popular but macabre features of this vast 14th century castle is a tour of the dungeon, where unfortunate prisoners were left to rot in isolation. Much of the castle is littered with "authentic" waxwork figures of royalty, courtesy of the castle's new owners, Madame Tussauds.

4 Leamington Spa

Like many of England's spa towns, Leamington Spa rose to prominence in the 18th century. The Royal Pump Room is still used for its original purpose, as a place to take medicinal waters and various spa treatments.

5 Althorp

This 16th century mansion may have passed unnoticed among England's many stately homes had it not been the childhood home of Lady Diana Spencer, later Princess of Wales. She is buried on a small island in a lake, which is not accessible to tourists. Her brother, Earl Spencer, has built in her memory a museum which is open each summer.

Local attractions/events:

Open all year (except some public holidays) unless otherwise shown

Surrounding areas:
(also refer to pages 131 & 133)

Stoneleigh Abbey, *Leamington Spa:* re-opening in 2000 after two years of renovation work, it is one of the finest country houses in the Midlands – magnificent staterooms and Chapel, medieval gatehouse and Regency stables

Wellsbourne Watermill, *Warwick:* award-winning historic watermill with one of the country's largest wooden waterwheels, and the chance to taste scones and cakes baked with the mill's own flour *(Apr-Sep)*

Hatton Country World, *Warwick:* a unique combination of leisure and shopping, carved out of 19th century farm buildings

Lord Leycester Hospital, *Warwick:* a group of 14th century timber-framed buildings which include the Great Hall, Galleries, Guildhall and Chantry Chapel, some of which have been used as locations in several major television productions *(Apr-Nov)*

Racecourse, *Warwick:* flat and jump fixtures throughout the year

Canon Ashby House, *Daventry:* the Dryden family home since the 1550s, it is one of the most romantic houses in the area, with Elizabethan wall paintings, sumptuous Jacobean plasterworks, medieval church and beautiful gardens *(Mar-Oct)*

British Waterways, *Solihull:* explore the nation's working industrial heritage through a network of canals

Baddesley Clinton Hall, *Solihull:* dating from the 14th century and little changed since 1634, this moated manor house also has romantic gardens, lake walks and nature trails *(Feb-Dec)*

Packwood House, *Solihull:* a 16th century house, which has been much altered over the years, it displays fine collections of textiles and furniture *(Mar-Oct)*

Heritage Hotels – Ullswater

Leeming House

Watermillock, Ullswater, Nr Penrith, Cumbria CA11 0JJ *See map page 10*
Tel:(0)870 400 8131 Fax:(0)17684 86443 General Manager: Christopher Curry
E-mail: HeritageHotels.Leeming_House@forte-hotels.com
Reservations: (0)870 400 8855 www.heritage-hotels.com

How to get there:

Leave the M6 and then follow the A66 and the A592 to Ullswater and Windermere. Soon you will reach Watermillock by Ullswater. The hotel is about 2 miles further on.

Facilities: 39 bedrooms, 1 mini-suite, 24-hour room service, hairdryer, trouser press, satellite TV, the Regency Restaurant, Conservatory, cocktail bar, private dining, drawing room, library and sitting room, open log fires in winter, garden, croquet lawn, private fishing, helipad, car park.
Family: Baby listening, baby sitting.

Leisure rates pppn

Midweek:	BB	DBB
Apr–Oct 2000	£ 69	£ 94
Nov–Feb	£ 49	£ 74
March 2001	£ 59	£ 84
Weekend:	BB	DBB
Apr–Oct 2000	£ 79	£104
Nov–Feb	£ 59	£ 84
March 2001	£ 69	£ 94

Lakeland Discovered Break rates

Price per person for two nights
May–October 2000
Fri/Sat–£330 Sun/Thur–£280
November 2000–April 2001
Fri/Sat–£280 Sun/Thur–£260
Upgrade to rooms with private balcony and overlooking gardens towards the lake £15 supplement per person per night
Please quote 'Special Break' when booking.

Once the private residence of the local Bolton family, this 200-year-old estate is surrounded by 20 acres of lush gardens in the heart of the glorious Lake District countryside. The Regency Restaurant, with its modern and classic menu that specialises in local produce, was chosen as the 1999 Lake District Restaurant of the Year.

Lakeland Discovered Break:

The tranquil and relaxing charms of Lake Ullswater await on a two-night break at this special country house hotel, a world away from the commercial pressures of everyday life and yet only seven miles from the M6 motorway.

The hotel is set in its own 20 acres of gardens, leading to the famous water where Wordsworth discovered his daffodils, and the endangered red squirrel can be frequently spotted.

Your room on arrival will have champagne, flowers, chocolates and bathrobes.

Dinner will be a relaxing affair with award-winning cuisine provided by our chef, Adam Marks, followed by coffee and petits fours in one of lounges.

Following breakfast, transportation to Windermere is arranged, where you will join some fellow explorers on a journey over the high and twisting passes of the Western Fells. With lots of stops throughout the day

you will enjoy visits to locations such as Hardknott Roman Forte, Eskdale, Wasdale and Muncaster Castle Gardens and Owl Sanctuary. There is also a train ride on the famous miniature railway at Eskdale. A gourmet dinner, prepared specially, with wine, awaits your return, then perhaps a stroll around the gardens to close the day.

Breakfast prior to departure with a last chance to explore before your journey home.

What's included in your break:
• 2 nights' dinner, bed and breakfast
• champagne, chocolates and flowers
• full-day excursion in west Cumbria
• ride on Ravensglass & Eskdale steam railway
• admission to Muncaster Castle Gardens and Owl Sanctuary
• 1 bottle house wine per couple on second night

Ullswater – Cumbria

1 Ullswater

The meandering lake is one of the most scenic in the region. The Ullswater Steamers cross the lake between Glenridding and Pooley Bridge, and it is a popular means of transport with both tourists and locals. *(Mar-Oct)*

3 Helvellyn

This 3000ft mountain is one of the more popular hikes in the Lake District. The climb is steep and rocky, but the views across the region from the summit make the effort worthwhile.

4 Penrith

Penrith Castle is now little more than a ruin, but its existence illustrates the importance of this town in the 14th century, when it was constantly under threat from its northern neighbours.

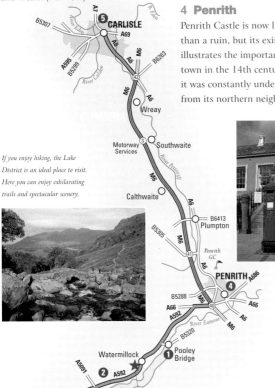

If you enjoy hiking, the Lake District is an ideal place to visit. Here you can enjoy exhilarating trails and spectacular scenery.

Commemorative red pillar box in front of the Old Town Hall, Carlisle.

5 Carlisle

Queen Elizabeth I imprisoned Mary, Queen of Scots in Carlisle Castle in the 16th century. The town has traditionally been a warring point between England and Scotland. The details of this period, and its earlier Roman history, are explained in the town's own museum.

In the centre of town is a beautiful 18th century Old Town Hall.

2 Gowbarrow Park

The most famous sight in this lakeside park can be seen in the spring, when the land bursts into bloom in a carpet of daffodils. William Wordsworth, the poet dedicated his most famous work to the flower.

Local attractions/events:

Open all year (except some public holidays) unless otherwise shown

Surrounding areas:
(also refer to pages 87 & 143)

Lowther Leisure and Wildlife Park: an all day attraction for the family in the natural beauty of the 150 acre park, including the famous Stevenson's Crown Circus *(Apr-Sept)*

Settle – Carlisle Railway, Appleby: England's most scenic railway, consisting of 72 miles of track, 20 major viaducts and 14 tunnels. A journey through the dramatic and inspiring countryside of the Yorkshire Dales and the lush Eden Valley

Penrith Museum: set in a 300 year old school, it details the area's fascinating past

Dalemain House & Gardens, *nr Penrith:* home to the Hassell family since 1679, it has fascinating interiors filled with fine furniture, family portraits and ceramics *(Apr-Oct)*

Brayham Castle, *nr Penrith:* these impressive ruins of a 13th century fortress, situated on the banks of the river Eamont, offer extensive views and a lively exhibition *(Apr-Oct)*

Hutton-in-the-Forest, *nr Penrith:* romantic and historic home of Lord and Lady Inglewood, dating from the 14th century, featuring fine collections of furniture, tapestries, portraits and ceramics *(Apr-Oct)*

Rheged Discovery Centre, *nr Penrith:* the newest and most inspiring attraction in the Lake District. A large format film complex will take you through 2000 years of Cumbria's history, mystery and magic

Carlisle Cathedral: founded in 1222, its glories include the East Window, the Brougham Triptych *(a 16th century Flemish altarpiece)* and notable examples of medieval carving

139

Heritage Hotels – Winchester

The Wessex

Paternoster Row, Winchester, Hampshire SO23 9LQ *See map page 4*
Tel: (0)870 400 8126 Fax: (0)196 284 1503 General Manager: James Leeming
E-mail: HeritageHotels_Winchester.Wessex@forte-hotels.com
Reservations: (0)870 400 8855 www.heritage-hotels.com

How to get there:
Take the M3 and leave at junction 9. Turn left into the one-way system, stay in the left-hand lane and then right

at the next roundabout into Broadway. Turn left into Colebrook Street and the Wessex is on your right.

Facilities: 91 bedrooms, 3 suites, 24-hour room service, hairdryer, digital TV, restaurant, lounge bar, free car parking *(for residents)*.

Family: Baby listening, baby sitting by prior arrangement.

Leisure rates pppn

Midweek:	BB	DBB
Apr 2000	£ 69	£ 84
May–Jun	£ 79	£ 94
Jul–Aug	£ 69	£ 84
Sep–Nov	£ 79	£ 94
Dec–Mar 2001	£ 69	£ 84
Weekend:	BB	DBB
Apr 2000	£ 59	£ 74
May–Jun	£ 69	£ 84
Jul–Aug	£ 59	£ 74
Sep–Nov	£ 69	£ 84
Dec–Mar 2001	£ 59	£ 74

A King Alfred's Connoisseur Break rates

£185 per person Apr–Oct,
£165 per person Nov–Mar 2001
Please quote 'Special Break' when booking.

The Wessex overlooks Winchester's magnificent 900-year-old cathedral, where the famous remains laid to rest include St Swithin, Jane Austen and many of the ancient kings of England. Its central location is ideally suited for strolling and soaking up the historic atmosphere of this city. Hardy, Trollope and Keats all spent time in Winchester and included the city in their writings. The William Walker Restaurant serves quality fresh food, and the cream teas are a high spot of the afternoons. Visit Winchester College or shop for antiques in Jewry Street. There is also good fishing in the local area.

A King Alfred's Connoisseur Break:

With the thousandth anniversary of King Alfred, we are delighted to offer a special heritage treat. Arrive on Friday and enjoy the comforts of a feature room overlooking the cathedral, with a welcome gift of champagne and chocolates and a guidebook to the city and Winchester Trail. Savour dinner in the candlelit restaurant, followed by a complimentary liqueur with your coffee. On Saturday explore the city on a conducted walking tour, and in the afternoon visit the cathedral, returning to the hotel for a full traditional tea in the lounge. In the evening, dine to the sounds of the pianist in the restaurant. On your way home on Sunday, visit The White Hart hotel, and experience a traditional Sunday lunch in the city of Salisbury.

What's included in your break:
• 2 nights' dinner, bed and breakfast
• a welcome gift of champagne and chocolates
• a guidebook to the city and Winchester Trail
• 3-course dinner from the full à la carte menu *(wine not included)*
• full English breakfast both days
• conducted walking tour of Winchester
• full traditional tea *(Saturday)*
• traditional Sunday Lunch at the White Hart

Winchester – Hampshire

1 Winchester Cathedral

The cathedral in this Roman city dates from 1079, but was not completed until the 14th century. Its most remarkable features are its nave – the longest in Europe – the crypt, which houses the tomb of St Swithun, and the marble font.

Town cryer outside Winchester Cathedral.

2 Avington Park

Although its origins stem from the Tudor period, the rooms on view in this mansion are uniquely decorated and painted from the Georgian era. In a lovely parkland setting, it offers supurb vistas with the chance to enjoy 'tea' in the orangery. *(May-Sep)*

The HMS Victory at Portsmouth. A visit on board reveals the often harsh existence of life at sea in the 18th and 19th centuries.

3 Watercress Line

The area around the town of Alresford was once used to grow watercress, hence the quaint name of this equally charming steam railway, part of the Mid-Hants Railway. The ten mile journey to Alton includes a four-course dinner at weekends.

4 Portsmouth

Once a great naval port, much of its historical treasures are dedicated to the memory of Lord Nelson and his conquests like the Battle of Trafalgar in 1805. His flagship, the HMS Victory, is permanently on display here, together with the 16th century Mary Rose.

5 Isle of Wight

A short ferry crossing will take you across to Cowes, noted for its annual yachting festival *(first week of August)* whilst nearby is Osborne House, commissioned by Prince Albert in 1845 to serve as the royal family's country home. It was here that Queen Victoria passed away in 1901.

Local attractions/events:

Open all year (except some public holidays) unless otherwise shown

Winchester:

College: The oldest school in England, founded in 1382 by Bishop William of Wykeham *(Apr-Sep)*

Museum Services: combining a number of interesting and historic venues – The City Museum, The Westgate and The Guildhall Gallery

Historic Resources Centre: headquarters of the Museum Services, located in a 17th century building, near to the site of Hyde Abbey, King Alfred's last known burial place

The Brooks Experience: view life as it would have been in Roman and Medieval Winchester. Based on actual excavated remains it tells the story through exciting action and drama

Wolvesey Castle: this extensive ruin was once one of the greatest medieval buildings in England, and the scene of the wedding in 1554 between Philip of Spain and Mary Tudor *(Apr-Oct)*

Cheyney Court: one of the most photographed scenes in Winchester, formerly the Bishop's court house

Surrounding areas:

(also refer to pages 85, 121 & 127)

Marwell Zoological Park, nr Winchester: world famous for its dedication to the conservation of endangered species, there are nearly 1000 animals in over a 100 acres of beautiful parkland

Silk Mill, Whitchurch: unique working museum delightfully situated on the River Test and still producing high quality silk fabrics on antique machinery

Wooldings Vineyard and Winery, Whitchurch: take the highly praised self-guided audio tour *(May-Dec)*

A Murder Mystery Weekend hotel – see pages 34-37

141

Heritage Hotels – Windermere

The Old England

Bowness-on-Windermere, Cumbria LA23 3DF *See map page 10*
Tel: (0)870 400 8130 Fax: (0)15394 43432 Regional General Manager: Colin Campbell
E-mail: HeritageHotels_Windermere.Old_England@forte-hotels.com
Reservations: (0)870 400 8855 www.heritage-hotels.com

How to get there:

The Old England is situated at the junction of the A5074 and the A592 on the shores of Windermere, about 18 miles from junction 36 of the M6.

Facilities: 72 bedrooms, 4 suites, hairdryer, trouser press, restaurant, bar, lounge, heated outdoor pool *(May–September)*, billiard room, garden, hair salon, free car park.
Family: Baby listening, baby sitting.

Leisure rates pppn

Midweek:	BB	DBB
Apr 2000	£ 50	£ 60
May–Oct	£ 60	£ 70
Nov–Feb	£ 44	£ 54
March 2001	£ 50	£ 60
Weekend:	**BB**	**DBB**
Apr 2000	£ 68	£ 78
May–Oct	£ 75	£ 85
Nov–Feb	£ 54	£ 64
March 2001	£ 68	£ 78

Above and Below the Lake District rates

Price per person for two nights (based on two sharing)
May 2000–Apr 2001
Fri/Sat–£190
Sun/Thur–£160
Lake view rooms supplement £15 per person per night

Please quote 'Special Break' when booking.

On the shores of England's largest lake, the Old England boasts unrivalled views of Windermere. This elegant Victorian mansion, superbly furnished with fine antiques, is ideally situated for bustling Bowness. Enjoy a drink in the bar, then dinner in the candlelit Vinand Restaurant, which provides a panoramic view as well as fine fare. Gardens (with outdoor games of draughts) lead down to the hotel's own jetties.

Above and Below the Lake District:

On arrival there will be champagne and chocolates in your room. Dinner will be served to the accompaniment of the resident pianist, while you watch the activities on the lake until nightfall. After breakfast you can board one of the Windermere Lake cruises, where you may venture to the small village of Ambleside. Stop here for a while and/or continue your journey back to Lakeside, where you will discover the Aquarium of the Lakes. Meet the UK's largest collection of freshwaterfish, including the predatory pike, encounter mischievous otters and meet sharks and rays from around the local coast. Not to be missed is the walk on Windermere's recreated lake bed to marvel at the diving ducks.
Bustling Bowness has many shops and your break includes a trip to the World of Beatrix Potter exhibition, while the jetties and the bay are just around the corner from the hotel.
In the summer months the Lakeside and Haverthwaite steam train will take you on a journey through contrasting lake and river scenes of the Leven Valley. Board one of the boats to return at your leisure to the hotel. Back at the hotel dinner is served in the award-winning Vinand restaurant. Breakfast prior to departure, then a last chance to explore before your journey home.

What's included in your break:
• 2 nights' dinner, bed and breakfast (wine not included)
• champagne and chocolates
• trip to Beatrix Potter World
• lake cruise to Ambleside
• entry to Aquarium of the Lakes
• return cruise on the lake

142

Windermere – Cumbria

1 Windermere

One of the most entertaining venues in this highly popular location is the Steamhouse Museum which recounts its national heritage and exhibits old steamers formerly used to navigate the lakes *(Mar-Oct)*. Lake cruises operate throughout most of the year.

Steamer on Lake Windermere.

3 Brantwood

Home of John Ruskin *(1872-1900)* Brantwood is one of the most beautifully situated houses in the Lake District. It contains a superb collection of Ruskin's drawings, water colours and personal items, more of which can be seen in the nearby Ruskin Museum *(Apr-Nov)*. Coniston Water is also famous for the world-speed records that have been set here.

4 Beatrix Potter Gallery

An annually changing exhibition of watercolours, illustrations and manuscripts by the celebrated children's author – just one of the many attractions dedicated to this pioneering Lake District lady.

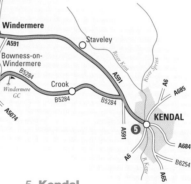

2 Ambleside

The picturesque harbour on Lake Windermere makes an attractive stop-off point, where you can watch the many amateur sailors who moor their boats here.

The 13th century church at Kendal.

5 Kendal

Regarded as the southern gateway to the Lake District, Kendal has remained true to its character as a working town rather than a tourist centre. Arthur Ransome, author of the children's classic *Swallows and Amazons*, worked in Kendal and is featured in the town's museum. Kendal is also known for its mint cake, an extremely sugary peppermint flavoured snack.

Local attractions/events:

Open all year (except some public holidays) unless otherwise shown

Windermere:

Lakeside & Haverthwaite Railway: steam locomotives haul comfortable coaches through the beautiful Leven Valley, where connections are available to other attractions *(Mar-Oct)*

Brockhole Visitor Centre: the first stop for visitors to the Lake District. Interactive exhibitions, audio visual presentations and a great insight into the 'beginnings' of this area and its history *(Mar-Nov)*

Surrounding areas:

(also refer to pages 87 & 139)

Stott Park Bobbin Mill, Newby Bridge: a genuine 19th century working mill – one of the best preserved in the country *(Apr-Oct)*

Aquarium of the Lakes, Newby Bridge: the Lake District's only underwater tunnel, featuring the UK's largest collection of freshwater fish, including sharks and rays

Holker Hall & Gardens, Grange Over Sands: award-winning gardens and also home to the Lakeland Motor Museum *(Apr-Oct)*

Sjergh Castle & Garden, nr Kendal: the pele tower dates from the 14th century but there is also a fine collection of Elizabethan furniture and portraits *(Apr-Oct)*

Levens Hall & Topiary Gardens, nr Kendal: Elizabethan mansion with the world famous gardens first laid out in 1694 – the location for the BBC drama 'Wives and Daughters' *(Apr-Oct)*

Quaker Tapestry Exhibition Centre, nr Kendal: an exhibition with illustrations by over 4000 men, women and children from 15 countries, exploring the Quaker journey from the 17th century to the present day *(Apr-Oct)*

A Murder Mystery Weekend hotel – see pages 34-37

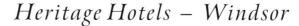

Heritage Hotels – Windsor

The Castle Hotel

High Street, Windsor, Berkshire SL4 1LJ *See map page 4*
Tel: (0)870 400 8300. Fax: (0)1753 830244
E-mail: HeritageHotels_Windsor.Castle@forte-hotels.com
Reservations: (0)870 400 8855 www.heritage-hotels.com

How to get there:
Leave the M4 at junction 6 and follow the signs for Windsor Castle. The hotel is in the High Street.

Facilities: 90 bedrooms, 4 four-posters, 3 suites, 14 executive rooms, 24-hour room service, hairdryer, trouser press, satellite TV, Castle Restaurant, Freshfields Restaurant, the Windsor Bar, the Pennington Lounge, original Georgian ballroom with extensive conference facilities. free car park.
Heathrow Airport in 25 minutes. 50 minutes direct rail to London.
Family: Baby listening, baby sitting.

Leisure rates pppn

Midweek:	BB	DBB
Apr–Jun	£ 95	£110
Jul–Aug	£ 85	£100
Sep–Nov	£ 95	£110
Dec–Feb 2001	£ 90	£110
Mar	£ 95	£110
Weekend:	BB	DBB
Apr–Mar 2001	£ 55	£ 75

Special Break rates
May–November
£205 per person for two nights
December–April
£190 per person for two nights
Upgrade to suite
£50 per person for two nights
Please quote 'Special Break' when booking.

Royal watchers get a bonus when they find out that this fine old Georgian hotel overlooks aspects of Windsor Castle and provides one of the finest views of the Changing of the Guard. Survey the dazzling ritual while taking morning coffee with teacakes or indulging in cream teas in the lounge. Of all the opulent bedrooms and superb suites, the most in demand is the Ripley Suite, creaking with atmosphere, loaded with luxury and, be warned, booked far in advance.

Castle Break:

Steeped in centuries of rich history, the Castle Hotel enjoys the ideal setting from which to discover all the town's attractions and shops. On arrival at the Castle, settle into your superbly appointed bedroom prior to enjoying a welcome aperitif in the comfort of the Windsor Bar. A sumptuous three-course dinner with coffee awaits you in the award-winning Castle Restaurant. Enjoy a leisurely breakfast before you embark on a day discovering Windsor's rich royal history. From close to the castle's entrance, the Good Friday Coach Tour will take you on an enjoyable and educational tour of Windsor and Eton. Following a light lunch, it's a short walk across the way to discover the treasures of the world's largest and oldest inhabited castle.

On return to the Castle Hotel you will, no doubt, be ready to enjoy a splendid dinner and take the chance to recount the day's events. No need to rush your departure – following breakfast take time to enjoy the many other treasures of this unique town.

What's included in your break:
• 2 nights' dinner, bed and breakfast *(wine not included)*
• aperitifs prior to dinner each evening
• first day lunch in the Freshfields Restaurant
• Good Friday Guided Tour of Windsor
• entrance to Windsor Castle *(subject to Castle opening times. Tickets cannot be pre-booked therefore this will be credited to you)*

Windsor – Berkshire

1 Windsor Castle

A castle has stood on this site since Norman times. Highlights of a tour around the castle are the Queen's Ballroom and the wonderfully ornate and technically brilliant dolls' house constructed for Queen Mary. *(Mar-Oct)*

2 St George's Chapel

Royalists will enjoy visiting Windsor's chapel, where numerous monarchs are buried, including Henry VIII and Charles I, and its memorial for Prince Albert, erected by his grieving widow Queen Victoria. *(Mar-Oct)*

3 Eton College

Founded in 1440, it has educated numerous dignitaries and well-known names, who have been seen walking the picturesque streets in their black gowns. A museum recounts past students' achievements. *(Mar-Oct)*

4 Dorney Court

Built in 1440, with 14th and 16th century oak, beautiful 17th century lacquer furniture and over 400 years of family history, Dorney is the ancient word for 'Island of Bees' and is famed for its honey. *(Jun-Sep)*

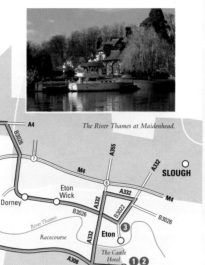

The River Thames at Maidenhead.

5 Maidenhead

Once an Edwardian centre of sophistication, stemming from champagne parties, fashionable events and Guards Club functions, it is now a thriving town of shops, restaurants and leisure activities. Discover Ray Mill Island with its ornamental gardens and fishpond, Brunel's Sounding Arch carrying the railway across the river, and Boulter's Lock – one of the prettiest locks on the Thames. Enjoy one of the many tour cruises on this stretch of the river, including a trip on the replica Victorian paddler, the *Lucy Fisher*, built for the Tarzan film *Greystoke*.

Local Attractions/events:

Open all year (except some public holidays) unless otherwise shown

Windsor:

Town & Crown Exhibition: includes audio visual presentations and display

The Changing of the Guard: it is part of daily life in the castle, with the exception of Sundays *(and weather permitting)*, the ceremony takes place outside the Guardroom in Lower Ward at 11am daily *(Apr-Aug)*

Frogmore House: beautiful gardens with the mausoleum of Queen Victoria and Albert, her Prince Consort *(limited opening)*

Horse Drawn Carriages: an elegant way to see more of the town

Brass Rubbing Centre: demonstrations and use of materials

Alexandra Gardens: an ideal spot for picnics in Spring/Summer

Polo at the Guards Club: an excellent way to spend a Sunday afternoon *(Apr-Sep)*

Theatre Royal: a full programme of varied productions

Racecourse: evening racing in summer is very popular *(Mar-Oct)*

Legoland: great fun for kids and adults alike *(Mar-Oct)*

Crooked House Tea Rooms: where better to rest your feet?

Royal Station Arcade: for notable fashion boutiques

River Thames Boat Trips: a truly relaxing way to see this stretch of the river *(Apr-Oct)*

Maidenhead:

Courage Shire Horse Centre: a great attraction for all the family

Cliveden House & Gardens: once the home of Lady Astor

Norden Farm Centre: arts and cultural activities *(opens May 2000)*

Cookham: enjoy one of many superb restaurants or visit the Stanley Spencer Gallery

145

Heritage Hotels – Woodstock

The Bear

Park Street, Woodstock, Oxfordshire OX20 1SZ *See map page 4*
Tel: (0)870 400 8202 Fax: (0)199 381 3380 Regional General Manager: James Stewart
E-mail: HeritageHotels_Woodstock.Bear@forte-hotels.com
Reservations: (0)870 400 8855 www.heritage-hotels.com

How to get there:

The Bear can be found beside the Town Hall, on Park Street, just off the High Street in the centre of Woodstock.

Facilities: 44 bedrooms, 6 four-posters, 4 suites, hairdryer, trouser press, David Garrick restaurant *(2 AA Rosettes)*, cocktail bar, lounge, open fires in winter, free parking *(limited)*.
Family: Baby listening, baby sitting.

Leisure rates pppn

Midweek:	BB	DBB
Apr–Jun 2000	£ 70	£ 85
Jul–Aug	£ 65	£ 80
Sep–Nov	£ 70	£ 85
Dec–Mar 2001	£ 75	£ 90
Weekend:	BB	DBB
Apr–Jun 2000	£ 75	£ 90
Jul–Aug	£ 70	£ 85
Sep–Feb	£ 75	£ 90
March 2001	£ 77	£ 92

Romantic Hideaway Break rates

Validity dates:
all dates until March 2001
Midweek: £240 pp for 2 nights
Weekend: £260 pp for 2 nights
Upgrade to a suite or four-poster room; £50 pp for 2 nights
(Rates for two people sharing; wine not included with meals.)
Please quote 'Special Break' when booking.

One of old England's original 13th-century coaching inns, 15 minutes from Oxford. A romantic hideaway, at one time a retreat for Elizabeth Taylor and Richard Burton during their long on-off love affair. Candlelight, oak beams, open fireplaces and dishes from around the world are served in the restaurant. There are good local leisure facilities and a varied selection of book and antiques shops.

Romantic Hideaway Break:

Dating back to the 13th century, the Bear at Woodstock is the ideal romantic hideaway hotel. Each of the bedrooms is full of character, with such features as fireplaces, oak beams and antiques. *(Richard Burton proposed to Elizabeth Taylor the second time in the Marlborough Suite!)*
The oak-beamed restaurant is candlelit every evening, while the tavern-style bar is a lovely place to have afternoon tea or just sit and read a book. For our Romantic Hideaway Break, chocolates, flowers and champagne await you in your room on your first evening. Enjoy a glass of champagne before a three-course dinner in the restaurant and finish your meal with a liqueur of your choice. The next morning, after a hearty English breakfast, you can join a walking tour of Royal Woodstock *(weekends only)*. You will also be issued with free entry to Blenheim Palace, the home of the Duke of Marlborough *(available only until the end of*

October – although the gardens designed by 'Capability' Brown are open throughout the year). The Palace is only three minutes' walk from the hotel. Enjoy dinner in the restaurant that evening with champagne and liqueurs, and retire to either your courtyard room or upstairs in the hotel. After breakfast the next morning you may want another stroll through Woodstock or drive to nearby Oxford *(15 minutes)*.

What's included in your break:
• 2 nights' dinner, bed and breakfast
• bathrobes, chocolates, champagne and flowers in the room on arrival
• a glass of champagne before dinner each evening and a liqueur to follow
• 2 full English breakfasts
• walking tour of Royal Woodstock *(weekends)*
• entrance to Blenheim Palace

Woodstock – Oxfordshire

1 Blenheim Palace

Queen Anne commissioned this baroque palace for the first Duke of Marlborough as a reward for his victory over the French in the Battle of Blenheim in 1704. Designed by John Vanbrugh, the palace was completed in 1722 and includes landscaped gardens and a lake. In 1874, the palace was the birthplace of Sir Winston Churchill. *(Mar-Oct)*

The magnificent Blenheim Palace was the birthplace of the former British prime minister, Sir Winston Churchill.

2 Cotswold Heritage Centre

Rural life, traditions and agricultural history are all on display in the unusual setting of a House of Correction, restored cell blocks and a courtroom. There is also a lifestyle exhibition of a typical household 'below stairs', with audio visual support.

3 Bourton-on-the-Water

A charming Cotswolds village, Bourton's beauty lies in its many miniature ornamental bridges crossing the River Windrush which flows through the town. A miniature model village showing the great buildings of the world is popular with children.

4 Stow-on-the-Wold

Stow is unique for its many narrow lanes, which all flow into the central market square – they were apparently designed so that sheep could be herded to market more easily. Today the lanes are lined with souvenir and antique shops.

Many of the older houses in the Cotswolds are built out of the local Cotswold stone.

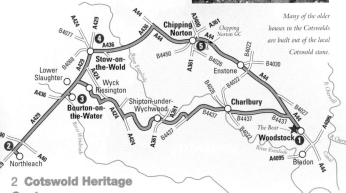

5 Chipping Norton

Having largely escaped the mass tourism of its neighbouring towns and villages, Chipping Norton is nevertheless worth a visit, particularly for its 17th century almshouses and its old Tweed Mill, now converted into luxury homes.

Local attractions/events:

Open all year (except some public holidays) unless otherwise shown

Surrounding areas:
(also refer to pages 53, 67, 117 & 131)

Cogges Manor Farm Museum, Witney: a working museum of Victorian rural life, farm buildings, traditional breeds of animals and exhibitions in the barns *(Mar-Oct)*

Medieval Bishops Palace, Witney: describes the political and religious role of the Bishop in the 12th and 13th centuries *(Apr-Sep)*

Keith Harding's World of Mechanical Music, Northleach: an award-winning museum of antique clocks, musical boxes, automata and mechanical musical instruments, introduced and played in the form of live entertainment in a period setting

Model Railway, Bourton-on-the-Water: over 400 square feet of the finest operating scenic model railway layouts in the country *(Feb-Dec)*

Cotswold Pottery, Bourton-on-the-Water: tucked away from the tourist track, the gallery displays a wide range of high quality, hand-made products

Miniature World, Bourton-on-the-Water: a new and fascinating indoor world with figures only 6 inches high. Incredible skills and craftsmanship – well worth a look! *(Mar-Oct)*

Model Village, Bourton-on-the-Water: built from Cotswold stone in 1937, it is a model of the actual village to ⅑ scale

Perfumery Exhibition, Bourton-on-the-Water: explores the origins and manufacture of perfume and includes 'smelly-vision' in a specially constructed cinema, Perfume Quiz and garden where you can experience the aromas

Prinknash Bird Park, Cranham: amongst the many peacocks and waterfowl, other attractions include the Golden Wood, the Love Bird Aviary, the Tudor wendy house and the Domed Aviary

IF YOU WANT TO GO BACK INTO HISTORY,
make sure you travel first class.

The Swan at Lavenham, one of Britain's finest medieval hotels, can be found just 78 miles from London, at the gateway to Constable country. Renowned designer Ann Boyd has recently completed a sensitive refurbishment of its 15th century interior, finding her inspiration in a series of wall paintings that were recently uncovered there.

The result is that heady mixture of old world charm, rich historical background and ultra modern facilities characteristic of every one of our unique hotels. Over 40 of these exquisite hideaways can be found across the country. To find the one for you, just call 0870 400 8855. Then you can be sure of leaving the 21st century in style.

HERITAGE HOTELS
www.heritage-hotels.com

Heritage Hotels – Website

We combine the best of our timeless hospitality with up to the minute information for all of your travel needs. Click into information on local events, places of interest, historic houses and museums, then book the Heritage Hotel of your choice.

www.heritage-hotels.com

Key to Maps

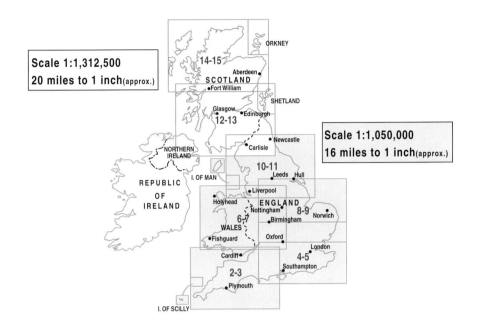

Scale 1:1,312,500
20 miles to 1 inch(approx.)

ORKNEY

14-15
Aberdeen
SCOTLAND
Fort William

SHETLAND

Glasgow
Edinburgh
12-13

Newcastle

Scale 1:1,050,000
16 miles to 1 inch(approx.)

NORTHERN
IRELAND

Carlisle

10-11
Leeds Hull

I. OF MAN

REPUBLIC
OF
IRELAND

Liverpool

Holyhead

ENGLAND
Nottingham
8-9
Birmingham
Norwich

6-7
WALES

Fishguard

Oxford

London

Cardiff

4-5
Southampton

2-3

Plymouth

I. OF SCILLY

Legend

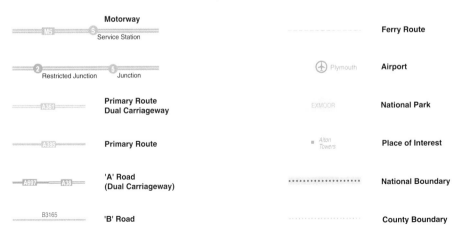

Motorway	Ferry Route
Service Station	
Restricted Junction Junction	Plymouth Airport
Primary Route Dual Carriageway	EXMOOR National Park
Primary Route	Alton Towers Place of Interest
'A' Road (Dual Carriageway)	National Boundary
B3165 'B' Road	County Boundary

© West One 2000

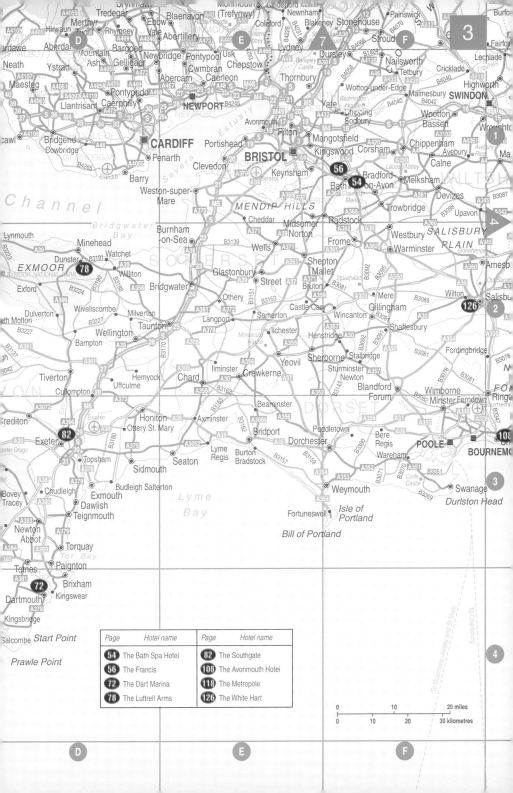

Page	Hotel name	Page	Hotel name
54	The Bath Spa Hotel	82	The Southgate
56	The Francis	108	The Avonmouth Hotel
72	The Dart Marina	118	The Metropole
78	The Luttrell Arms	126	The White Hart

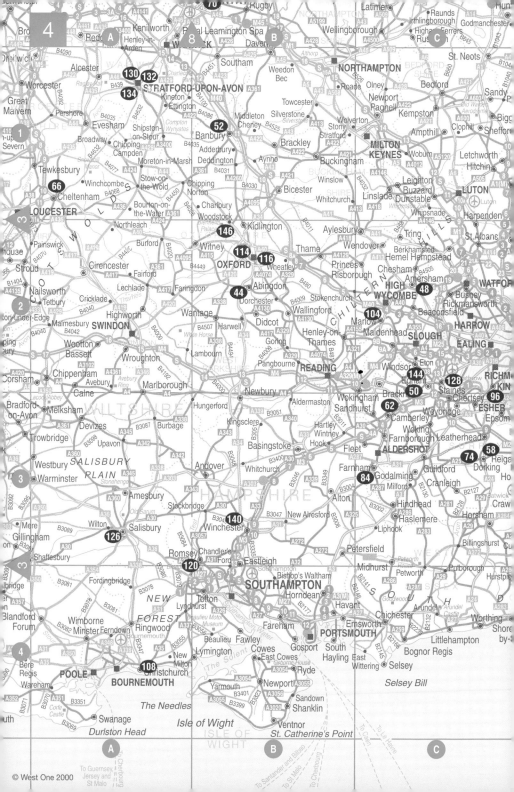

Page	Hotel name	Page	Hotel name
52	Whately Hall	**106**	The New Bath Hotel
66	The Queen's	**130**	The Alveston Manor
68	Blossoms Hotel	**132**	The Shakespeare
70	Brandon Hall	**134**	The Swan's Nest
76	Peveril of the Peak	**146**	The Bear

© West One 2000

Page	Hotel name	Page	Hotel name
52	Whately Hall	100	The White Hart
66	The Queen's	106	The New Bath Hotel
70	Brandon Hall	130	The Alveston Manor
76	Peveril of the Peak	132	The Shakespeare
92	The White Horse	134	The Swan's Nest
98	The Swan	146	The Bear

© West One, 2000

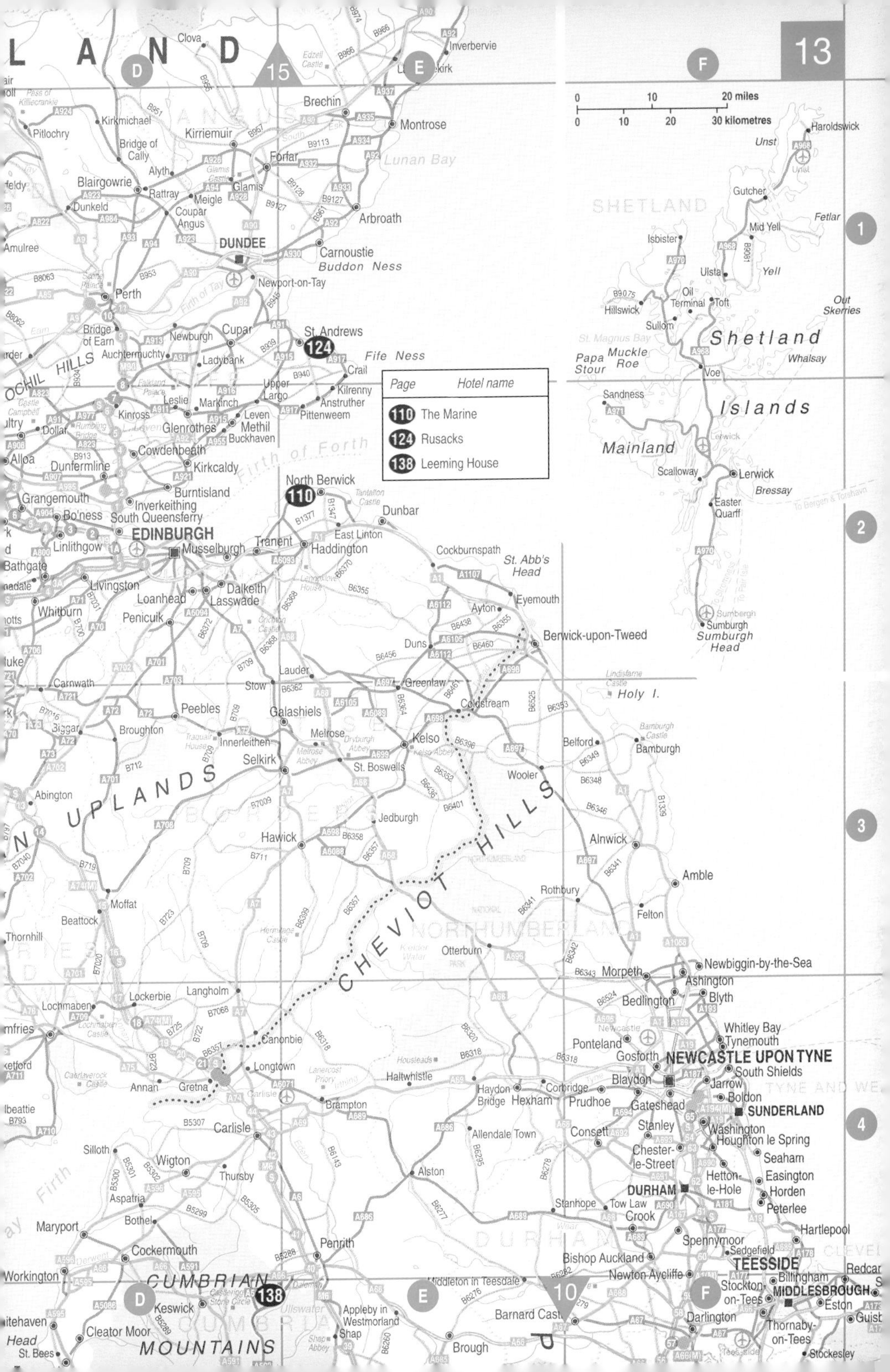

Page
Hotel name
110 The Marine
124 Rusacks
138 Leeming House
0 10 20 miles
0 10 20 30 kilometres
L A N D
OCHIL HILLS
UPLANDS
CHEVIOT HILLS
CUMBRIAN MOUNTAINS
SHETLAND
Shetland Islands
Mainland
Unst
Yell
Fetlar
Whalsay
Out Skerries
Papa Stour
Muckle Roe
Bressay
Haroldswick
Gutcher
Mid Yell
Isbister
Ulsta
Oil Terminal
Toft
Hillswick
Sullom
St. Magnus Bay
Voe
Sandness
Lerwick
Scalloway
Easter Quarff
Sumburgh
Sumburgh Head
To Bergen & Torshavn
Clova
Inverbervie
Edzell Castle
Brechin
Montrose
Lunan Bay
Kirkmichael
Pitlochry
Pass of Killiecrankie
Kirriemuir
Bridge of Cally
Forfar
Alyth
Glamis
Blairgowrie
Rattray
Meigle
Dunkeld
Coupar Angus
Arbroath
Amulree
DUNDEE
Carnoustie
Buddon Ness
Newport-on-Tay
Perth
Scone Palace
Firth of Tay
Bridge of Earn
Newburgh
Cupar
St. Andrews
Auchtermuchty
Ladybank
Fife Ness
Crail
Kilrenny
Anstruther
Pittenweem
Upper Largo
Leslie
Markinch
Falkland Palace
Kinross
Leven
Methil
Buckhaven
Glenrothes
Castle Campbell
Dollar
Rumbling Bridge
Alloa
Cowdenbeath
Dunfermline
Kirkcaldy
Firth of Forth
Burntisland
Grangemouth
Inverkeithing
Bo'ness
South Queensferry
North Berwick
Tantallon Castle
Dunbar
EDINBURGH
Linlithgow
Musselburgh
Tranent
Haddington
East Linton
Bathgate
Livingston
Cockburnspath
St. Abb's Head
Eyemouth
Lennoxlove House
Loanhead
Dalkeith
Lasswade
Whitburn
Penicuik
Crichton Castle
Ayton
Berwick-upon-Tweed
Duns
Lauder
Greenlaw
Carnwath
Stow
Coldstream
Lindisfarne Castle
Holy I.
Biggar
Peebles
Galashiels
Broughton
Traquair House
Innerleithen
Melrose
Dryburgh Abbey
Melrose Abbey
Kelso
Kelso Abbey
Belford
Bamburgh Castle
Bamburgh
Selkirk
St. Boswells
Wooler
Abington
Jedburgh
Hawick
Alnwick
NORTHUMBERLAND
Amble
Moffat
Rothbury
Felton
Beattock
NORTHUMBERLAND
Hermitage Castle
Thornhill
Kielder Water
Otterburn
Newbiggin-by-the-Sea
Morpeth
Ashington
Lockerbie
Langholm
Bedlington
Blyth
Lochmaben
Lochmaben Castle
Whitley Bay
Tynemouth
Canonbie
Newcastle
Ponteland
Gosforth
NEWCASTLE UPON TYNE
South Shields
Caerlaverock Castle
Longtown
Housesteads
Lanercost Priory
Haltwhistle
Jarrow
Annan
Gretna
Carlisle
Haydon Bridge
Hexham
Corbridge
Prudhoe
Blaydon
Boldon
Brampton
Gateshead
SUNDERLAND
Silloth
Allendale Town
Consett
Stanley
Washington
Houghton le Spring
Wigton
Chester-le-Street
Seaham
Thursby
Alston
Hetton-le-Hole
Easington
Horden
DURHAM
Aspatria
Stanhope
Tow Law
Crook
Peterlee
Maryport
Bothel
Spennymoor
Hartlepool
Cockermouth
Penrith
Bishop Auckland
Sedgefield
Workington
Newton Aycliffe
TEESSIDE
Billingham
Redcar
Middleton in Teesdale
Stockton-on-Tees
MIDDLESBROUGH
Eston
Keswick
Castlerigg Stone Circle
Ullswater
Appleby in Westmorland
Barnard Castle
Darlington
Guisborough
Whitehaven
Cleator Moor
Shap
Shap Abbey
Thornaby-on-Tees
St. Bees Head
St. Bees
Brough
Stokesley
Teesside
DURHAM
TYNE AND WEAR

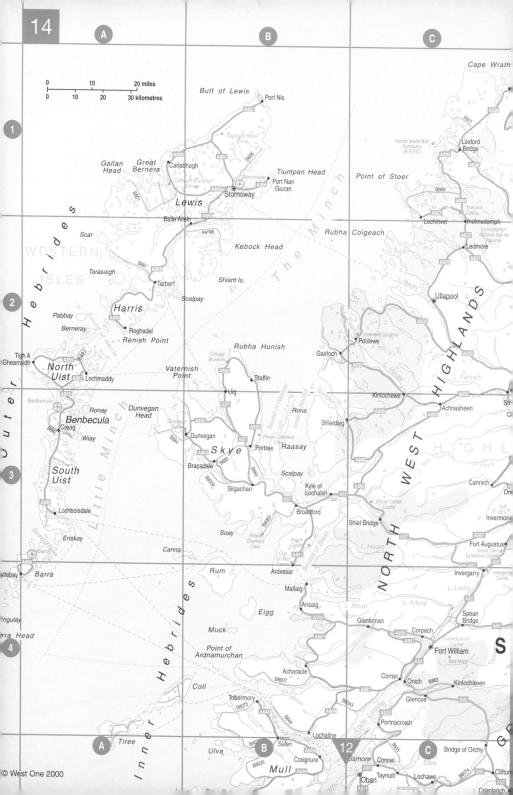

A

B

C

1

2

3

4

Cape Wrath

Butt of Lewis

Port Nis

A857

B801

Hando Island Bird
Sanctuary
(R.S.P.B.)

Laxford
Bridge

A838

A838

Cairn and Stone
Circle

A858

A859

B895

Gallan
Head

Great
Bernera

Carlabhagh

A857

B895

Tiumpan Head

Point of Stoer

A894

A837

A838

Callanish Standing
Stones

Stornoway

Port Nan
Giuran

B869

Ardvreck
Castle

Lochinver

Inchnadamph

A837

WESTERN

Scar

Lewis

A858

Stornoway

The

Inchnadamph
National Nature
Reserve

Ledmore

A835

A837

ISLES

Baile Ailein

B897

Kebock Head

Minch

Rubha Coigeach

Ullapool

HIGHLANDS

B887

Tarasaigh

Tarbert

Shiant Is.

L. Broom

Harris

Scalpay

Inverewe Gardens

Pabbay

A859

Roghadal

Renish Point

Rubha Hunish

Gairloch

Poolewe

A832

L. Fannich

Berneray

A832

Tigh A
Ghearraidh

B893

A867

North
Uist

Lochmaddy

Vaternish
Point

A855

Staffin

Kinlochewe

A896

Achnasheen

A832

A890

Str

Sound of Harris

Cottage
Museum

Uig

A87

Rona

Shieldaig

A896

Benbecula

A865

Ronay

Dunvegan
Head

A850

Dunvegan
Castle

Prince Charles's
Cave

HIGHL

Benbecula

Creag

B892

Wiay

Dunvegan

B884

A863

Skye

Bracadale

B885

Portree

Sound of Raasay

Raasay

Scalpay

A87

L. Torridon

Inner Sound

Farrat

Cannich

South
Uist

Little Minch

B8009

Sligachan

B862

B803

Kyle of
Lochalsh

A890

A87

Loc

Eilean Donan
Castle

Dru

Invermoris

Lochboisdale

A865

Broadford

Shiel Bridge

A87

Soay

Prince Charles's
Cave

Sound of Sleat

A851

Knock
Castle

Clan Donald
Centre

L. Hourn

Fort Augustus

Great Glen
Exhibition Centre

A82

Eriskay

Canna

Rum

Ardvasar

Invergarry

Invergarry
Castle

Barra

Castlebay

A888

Mallaig

Arisaig

L. Morar

L. Arkaig

L. Lochy

A82

Spean
Bridge

A86

ngulay

rra Head

Eigg

Glenfinnan

A830

A861

Corpach

A830

A861

Caledonian
Canal

S

Muck

Point of
Ardnamurchan

Acharacle

B8007

Corran

A861

Onich

A82

Fort William

Ben Nevis

B863

Kinlochleven

Coll

Tobermory

B8073

B849

A848

B8043

Glencoe

A82

Lochaline

Portnacroish

Loch Linnhe

A828

Tiree

Ulva

Salen

A849

Craignure

A848

12

Lismore

Connel

B845

Bridge of Orchy

GR

Mull

B8035

Oban

Taynuilt

Lochawe

B8074

A85

Clifton

Ardanaiseig

A816

Crianlarich

A

B

C

© West One 2000

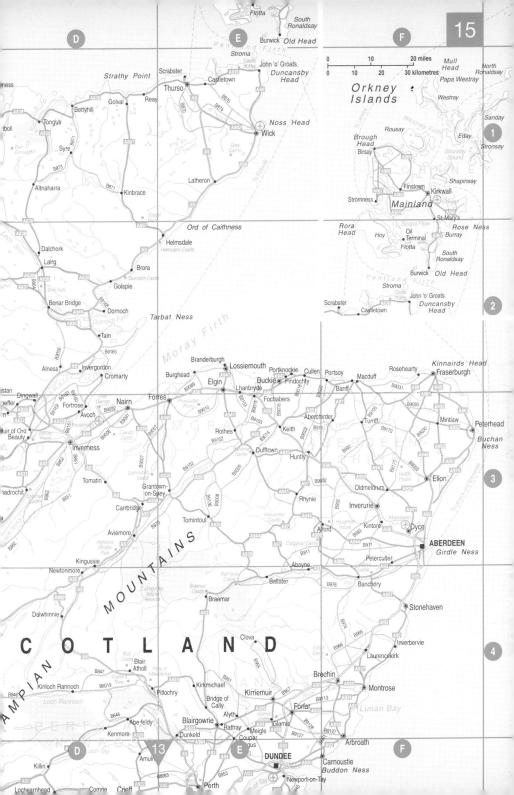

INDEX TO GREAT BRITAIN

Canterbury 5 E3
Canvey Island 5 E2
Capel Curig 6 C1
Cardiff 3 D1
Cardigan 6 B4
Carlabhagh 14 A1
Carlisle 10 B1
Carlton 8 B2
Carluke 12 C2
Carmarthen 6 B4
Carnforth 10 B3
Carnoustie 13 E1
Carnwath 13 D3
Carrbridge 15 D3
Carsphairn 12 C3
Castle Cary 3 E2
Castle Donington 8 B2
Castle Douglas 12 C4
Castlebay 14 A4
Castleford 11 D
Castletown (High) 15 E1
Castletown (IoM) 10 A4
Catel 2 A2
Caterham 5 D3
Catterick Camp 10 C2
Chandler's Ford 4 B3
Chard 3 E2
Charing 5 E3
Charlbury 4 B1
Chatham 5 E2
Chatteris 9 D3
Cheadle (G Man) 10 C4
Cheadle (Staf) 7 F2
Cheddar 3 E1
Chelmsford 5 D2
Cheltenham 7 E4
Chepstow 3 E1
Chertsey 4 C3
Chesham 4 C2
Cheshunt 5 D2
Chester 7 D1
Chesterfield 8 B1
Chester-le Street 11 D1
Chichester 4 C4
Chippenham 3 F1
Chipping Campden 4 A1
Chipping Norton 4 A1
Chipping Ongar 5 D2
Chipping Sodbury 3 F1
Chirk 7 D2
Chorley 10 B4
Christchurch 4 A4
Chudleigh 3 D3
Chumleigh 2 C2
Church Stretton 7 D3
Cinderford 7 E4
Cirencester A2
Clachan 12 B2
Clacton-on-Sea 5 E1
Claonaig 12 B2
Cleator Moor 10 A2
Cleethorpes 11 F4
Cleobury Mortimer 7 E3
Clevedon 3 E1
Cleveleys 10 B3
Clifton 12 C1
Cliftonville 5 F2
Clitheroe 10 C3
Clophill 4 C1
Clova 15 E4
Clovelly 2 C2
Clun 7 D3
Clydebank 12 C2
Coalville 8 B3
Cockburnspath 13 E2
Cockermouth 10 A1
Coggeshall 5 E1
Colchester 5 E1

Coldstream 13 E3
Coleford 7 E4
Colne 10 C3
Colwyn Bay 6 C1
Combe Martin 2 C2
Comrie 12 C1
Congleton 7 E1
Conisbrough 11 D4
Coniston 10 B2
Connel 12 B1
Consett 10 C1
Contin 15 D3
Conwy 6 C1
Corbridge 10 C1
Corby Glen 8 C2
Corby 8 C3
Corpach 14 C4
Corran 12 B1
Corsham 3 F1
Corton 9 F3
Corwen 7 D2
Coryton 5 E2
Cottenham 9 D4
Cottesmore 8 C3
Coulport 12 B2
Coupar Angus 13 D1
Coventry 7 F3
Cowbridge 3 D1
Cowdenbeath 13 D2
Cowes 4 B4
Craighouse 12 A2
Craignure 12 A1
Crail 13 E1
Cranbrook 5 E3
Cranleigh 4 C3
Cranwell 8 C2
Craven Arms 7 D3
Crawley 5 D3
Cray Cross 8 B2
Creag 14 A3
Crediton 3 E1
Crewe 7 E1
Crewkerne 3 E2
Crianlarich 12 C1
Criccieth 6 B2
Cricklade 4 A2
Crieff 12 C1
Crocketford 12 C4
Cromarty 15 D2
Cromer 9 F2
Crook 10 C1
Crosby 10 B4
Crowborough 5 D3
Crowland 8 C3
Crowle 11 E4
Croxton Kerrial 8 B2
Croydon 5 D3
Cuckfield 5 D3
Cullen 15 E2
Cullompton 3 D2
Cumbernauld 12 C2
Cumnock 12 C3
Cupar 13 D1
Cwmbran 3 E1

D

Dalbeattie 12 C4
Dalchork 15 D2
Dale 6 A4
Dalkeith 13 D2
Dalmellington 12 C3
Dalry 12 C2
Dalton-in-Furness 10 A3
Dalwhinnie 15 D4
Darlington 11 D2
Dartford 5 D2
Dartmeet 2 C3
Dartmouth 3 D4

Darvel 12 C3
Darwen 10 B4
Daventry 4 B1
Dawlish 3 D3
Deal 5 F3
Deddington 4 B1
Denbigh 7 D1
Denny 12 C2
Derby 7 F1
Desborough 8 B3
Devizes 4 A3
Dewsbury 11 D4
Didcot 4 B2
Dinas-Mawddwy 6 C2
Dingwall 15 D3
Dinnington 11 D4
Diss 9 E3
Dolgellau 6 C2
Dollar 13 D2
Doncaster 11 D4
Donington 8 C2
Dorchester (Dor) 3 F3
Dorchester (Oxon) 4 B2
Dorking 4 C3
Dornoch 15 D2
Douglas (IoM) 10 A4
Douglas (S Lan) 12 C3
Doune 12 C2
Dover 5 F3
Downham Market 9 D3
Droitwich 7 E3
Dronfield 8 B1
Drummore 12 B4
Drumnadrochit 15 D3
Drymen 12 C2
Duddington 8 C3
Dudley 7 E3
Dufftown 15 E3
Dulverton 3 D2
Dumbarton 12 C2
Dumfries 10 A1
Dunbar 13 E2
Dunblane 12 C2
Dundee 13 D1
Dunfermline 13 D2
Dunkeld 13 D1
Dunoon 12 B2
Duns 13 E2
Dunstable 4 C1
Dunster 3 D2
Dunvegan 14 B3
Durham 11 D1
Durness 14 C1
Dursley 3 F1
Dyce 15 F3
Dyffryn 6 B1

E

Ealing 4 C2
Eardisley 7 D3
Easington (Dur) 11 D1
Easington (E York) 11 F4
Easingwold 11 D3
East Bergholt 5 E1
East Cowes 4 B4
East Dereham 9 E3
East Grinstead 5 D3
East Kilbride 12 C2
East Linton 13 E2
East Retford 8 B1
East Wittering 4 C4
Eastbourne 5 D4
Easter Quarff 13 F2
Eastleigh 4 B3
Ebbw Vale 7 D4
Eccleshall 7 E2
Eckington 8 B1
Edenbridge 5 D3

Edinburgh 13 D2
Egham 4 C2
Egremont 10 A2
Elgin 15 E2
Elland 10 C4
Ellesmere Port 7 D1
Ellesmere 7 D2
Ellon 15 F3
Ely 9 D3
Emsworth 4 B4
Epping 5 D2
Epsom 4 C3
Eribol 14 C1
Esher 4 C3
Eston 11 D2
Eton 4 C2
Ettington 4 A1
Evesham 4 A1
Exeter 3 D3
Exford 3 D2
Exmouth 3 D3
Eye 9 E3
Eyemouth 13 E2

F

Fairford 4 A2
Fakenham 9 E2
Falkirk 13 D2
Falmouth 2 B4
Fareham 4 B4
Faringdon 4 A2
Farnborough 4 C3
Farnham 4 C3
Farnworth 10 C4
Faversham 5 E3
Fawley 4 B4
Felixstowe 5 F1
Felton 13 F3
Feolin Ferry 12 A2
Ferndown 4 A4
Ffestiniog 6 C2
Filey 11 F2
Filton 3 E1
Findochty 15 E2
Finstown 15 F1
Fionnphort 12 A1
Fishguard 6 A4
Fleet 4 C3
Fleetwood 10 B3
Flint 7 D1
Fochabers 15 E3
Folkestone 5 F3
Fordingbridge 4 A4
Forfar 13 D1
Formby 10 B4
Forres 15 E3
Fort Augustus 14 C3
Fort William 14 C4
Fortrose 15 D3
Fortuneswell 3 F3
Fowey 2 B4
Framlingham 9 F4
Fraserburgh 15 F2
Fridaythorpe 11 E3
Frinton-on-Sea 5 F1
Frodsham 7 D1
Frome 3 F2
Furnace 12 B2

G

Gainsborough 11 E4
Gairloch 14 B2
Galashiels 13 E3
Galston 12 C3
Garelochhead 12 B2
Garstang 10 B3
Gatehouse of Fleet 12 C4
Gateshead 11 D1

Gelligaer 3 D1
Gillingham (Dor) 3 F2
Gillingham (Med) 5 E2
Girvan 12 B3
Gisburn 10 C3
Glamis 13 D1
Glasgow 12 C2
Glastonbury 3 E2
Glenbarr 12 A3
Glencoe 12 B1
Glenfinnan 14 C4
Glenluce 12 B4
Glenrothes 13 D2
Glossop 10 C4
Gloucester 7 E4
Godalming 4 C3
Godmanchester 8 C4
Godstone 5 D3
Golspie 15 D2
Golval 15 D1
Goodwick 6 A4
Goole 11 E4
Gorey 2 B2
Goring 4 B2
Gorstan 14 C2
Gosforth 11 D1
Gosport 4 B4
Gourock 12 B2
Grain 5 E2
Grangemouth 13 D2
Grange-over-Sands 10 B3
Grantham 8 C2
Grantown-on-Spey 15 E3
Grasmere 10 B2
Gravesend 5 D2
Grays 5 D2
Great Driffield 11 E3
Great Dunmow 5 D1
Great Malvern 7 E4
Great Shelford 5 D1
Great Torrington 2 C2
Great Yarmouth 9 F3
Greenlaw 13 E3
Greenock 12 B2
Greenod 10 B2
Gretna 10 B1
Grimsby 11 F4
Guildford 4 C3
Guisborough 11 D2
Gutcher 13 F1
Guyhirn 9 D3

H

Haddington 13 E2
Hadleigh 5 E1
Hagley 7 E3
Hailsham 5 D4
Halesowen 7 F3
Halesworth 9 F3
Halifax 10 C4
Halstead 5 E1
Haltwhistle 10 B1
Hamilton 12 C2
Hanley 7 E1
Harlech 6 C2
Harleston 9 F3
Harlow 5 D2
Haroldswick 13 F1
Harpenden 4 C2
Harrogate 11 D3
Harrow 4 C2
Hartland 2 B2
Hartlepool 11 D1
Hartley Wintney 4 B3
Harwell 4 B2
Harwich 5 F1
Haslemere 4 C3
Hastings 5 E4

Hatfield (Herts) 4 C2
Hatfield (S York) 11 E4
Hatherleigh 2 C3
Havant 4 B4
Haverfordwest 6 A4
Haverhill 5 D1
Hawarden 7 D1
Hawes 10 C2
Hawick 13 E3
Hawkhurst 5 E3
Hawkshead 10 B2
Haworth 10 C3
Haydon Bridge 10 C1
Hayle 2 A4
Hay-on-Wye 7 D4
Haywards Heath 5 D3
Heanor 8 B2
Heathfield 5 D3
Hebden Bridge 10 C4
Hedon 11 F4
Helensburgh 12 C2
Helmsdale 15 E2
Helmsley 11 D2
Helston 2 A4
Hemel Hempstead 4 C2
Hemyock 3 D2
Henley-in-Arden 7 F3
Henley-on-Thames 4 B2
Henstridge 3 F2
Hereford 7 E4
Herne Bay 5 E2
Hertford 5 D2
Hetton-le-Hole 11 D1
Hexham 10 C1
Heysham 10 B3
High Wycombe 4 C2
Higham Ferrers 8 C4
Highworth 4 A2
Hillswick 13 F1
Hinckley 8 B3
Hindhead 4 C3
Hirwaun 6 C4
Histon 9 D4
Hitchin 4 C1
Hoddesdon 5 D2
Hodnet 7 E2
Holbeach 9 D2
Holland-on-Sea 5 F1
Holmfirth 10 C4
Holmhead 12 C3
Holsworthy 2 C3
Holt 9 E2
Holyhead (Caergybi) 6 B1
Holywell 7 D1
Honiton 3 D3
Hook 4 B3
Hope 7 D1
Hopton 9 F3
Horden 11 D1
Horley 5 D3
Horncastle 8 C1
Horndean 4 B4
Hornsea 11 F3
Horsham 4 C3
Houghton le Spring 11 D1
Hounslow 4 C2
Hove 5 D4
Howden 11 E4
Hoylake 10 A4
Hucknall 8 B2
Huddersfield 10 C4
Hugh Town 2 A3
Hungerford 4 B3
Hunmanby 11 E3
Hunstanton 9 D2
Huntingdon 8 C4
Huntley 7 E4
Huntly 15 E3

Prestwick 12 C3
Preteigne 7 D3
Princes Risborough 4 C2
Prudhoe 10 C1
Puckeridge 5 D1
Puddletown 3 F3
Pudsey 11 D3
Pulborough 4 C4
Pwllheli 6 B2

Q
Queensferry 7 D1

R
Radstock 3 F1
Rainham 5 E3
Ramsey *(Camb)* 8 C3
Ramsey *(IoM)* 10 A4
Ramsgate 5 F3
Rattray 13 D1
Raunds 8 C4
Ravenglass 10 A2
Rawmarsh 11 D4
Rawtenstall 10 C4
Rayleigh 5 E2
Reading 4 B2
Reay 15 D1
Redcar 11 D2
Redditch 7 F3
Redhill 5 D3
Redruth 2 A4
Reepham 9 E2
Reigate 5 D3
Rhayader 6 C3
Rhosneigr 6 B1
Rhos-on-Sea 6 C1
Rhuddlan 6 C1
Rhyl 6 C1
Rhymney 7 D4
Rhynie 15 F3
Richmond 10 C2
Rickmansworth 4 C2
Ringwood 4 A4
Ripley 8 B2
Ripon 11 D3
Roade 4 B1
Robin Hood's Bay 11 E2
Rochdale 10 C4
Rochester 5 E2
Roghadal 14 A2
Romsey 4 B3
Rosehearty 15 F2
Ross-on-Wye 7 E4
Rothbury 13 F3
Rotherham 11 D4
Rothes 15 E3
Rothesay 12 B2
Rothwell *(North)* 8 C3
Rothwell *(W York)* 11 D4
Royal Leamington Spa
 7 F3
Royal Tunbridge Wells
 5 D3
Royston 5 D1
Rozel 2 B2
Rugby 8 B3
Rugeley 7 F2
Runcorn 7 E1
Rushden 8 C4
Ruthin 7 D1
Ryde 4 B4
Rye 5 E3

S
Saffron Walden 5 D1
Salcombe 2 C4
Sale 10 C4
Salen 12 A1

Salford 10 C4
Salisbury 4 A3
Saltash 2 C4
Saltburn-by-the-Sea
 11 E2
Saltcoats 12 B3
Sandbach 7 E1
Sandhead 12 B4
Sandhurst 4 C3
Sandness 13 F2
Sandown 4 B4
Sandringham 9 D2
Sandwich 5 F3
Sandy 4 C1
Sanquhar 12 C3
Saundersfoot 6 B4
Saxmundham 9 F4
Scalasaig 12 A2
Scalby 11 E2
Scalloway 13 F2
Scarborough 11 E2
Scrabster 15 E1
Scunthorpe 11 E4
Seaford 5 D4
Seaham 11 D1
Seascale 10 A2
Seaton 3 E3
Sedburgh 10 B2
Sedgefield 11 D1
Selby 11 D3
Selkirk 13 E3
Selsey 4 C4
Settle 10 C3
Sevenoaks 5 D3
Shaftesbury 3 F2
Shanklin 4 B4
Shap 10 B2
Sheerness 5 E2
Sheffield 11 D4
Shefford 4 C1
Shepshed 8 B3
Shepton Mallet 3 E2
Sherborne 3 E2
Sheringham 9 E2
Shiel Bridge 14 C3
Shieldaig 14 B3
Shifnal 7 E2
Shipley 10 C3
Shipston-on-Stour 4 A1
Shoeburyness 5 E2
Shoreham-by-Sea 4 C4
Shotley Gate 5 F1
Shotts 12 C2
Shrewsbury 7 D2
Sidmouth 3 D3
Silloth 10 A1
Silsden 10 C3
Silverstone 4 B1
Sittingbourne 5 E3
Skegness 9 D2
Skelmersdale 10 B4
Skipton 10 C3
Sleaford 8 C2
Sligachan 14 B3
Slough 4 C2
Soham 9 D3
Solihull 7 F3
Somerton 3 E2
South Cave 11 E3
South Hayling 4 B4
South Molton 2 C2
South Queensferry 13 D2
South Shields 11 D1
Southam 4 B1
Southampton 4 B3
Southborough 5 D3
Southend 12 A3
Southend-on-Sea 5 E2

Southport 10 B4
Southwell 8 B2
Southwold 9 F3
Sowerby Bridge 10 C4
Spalding 8 C2
Spean Bridge 14 C4
Spennymoor 11 D1
Spilsby 9 D2
St Agnes 2 A4
St Albans 4 C2
St Andrews 13 E1
St Anne 2 A1
St Asaph 7 D1
St Aubin 2 A2
St Austell 2 B4
St Bees 10 A2
St Boswells 13 E3
St Brelade 2 A2
St Clears 6 B4
St Clement 2 B2
St Columb Major 2 B3
St David's 6 A4
St Helens 10 B4
St Helier 2 A2
St Ives *(Camb)* 9 D4
St Ives *(Corn)* 2 A4
St Just 2 A4
St Keverne 2 A4
St Lawrence 2 A2
St Martin 2 A2
St Mary's 15 F1
St Mawes 2 B4
St Neots 4 C1
St Ouen 2 A2
St Peter 2 A2
St Peter Port 2 A2
St Sampson 2 A2
St Saviour *(Guer)* 2 A2
St Saviour *(Jer)* 2 B2
Staffin 14 B2
Stafford 7 E2
Staines 4 C2
Stalbridge 3 F2
Stalham 9 F2
Stamford Bridge 11 E3
Stamford 8 C2
Stanhope 10 C1
Stanley 11 D1
Stansted 5 D1
Staveley 8 B1
Stevenage 4 C1
Stevenston 12 B3
Stewarton 12 C3
Stilton 8 C3
Stirling 12 C2
Stockbridge 4 B3
Stockport 10 C4
Stocksbridge 11 D4
Stockton-on-Tees 11 D2
Stoke Ferry 9 D3
Stokenchurch 4 B2
Stoke-on-Trent 7 E1
Stokesley 11 D2
Stone 7 E2
Stonehaven 15 F4
Stonehouse 7 E4
Stony Stratford 4 B1
Stornoway 14 B1
Stourbridge 7 E3
Stourport-on-Severn 7 E3
Stow 13 D2
Stowmarket 5 E1
Stow-on-the-Wold 4 A1
Stranraer 12 B4
Stratford-upon-Avon 4 A1
Strathaven 12 C3
Strathpeffer 15 D3
Stratton 2 B2

Street 3 E2
Stromness 15 F1
Stroud 7 E4
Sturminster Newton 3 F2
Sudbury *(Derb)* 7 F2
Sudbury *(Suff)* 5 E1
Sullom 13 F1
Sumburgh 13 F2
Sunderland 11 D1
Sutterton 9 D2
Sutton Coldfield 7 F2
Sutton in Ashfield 8 B2
Sutton on Sea 9 D1
Swadlincote 7 F2
Swaffham 9 E3
Swanage 4 A4
Swansea 2 C1
Swinderby 8 C2
Swindon 4 A2
Swineshead 8 C2
Syre 15 D1
Syston 8 B3

T
Tadcaster 11 D3
Tain 15 D2
Tamworth 7 F2
Tarbert *(Arg)* 12 B2
Tarbert *(W Isl)* 14 A2
Tarbet 12 C2
Tarporley 7 E1
Taunton 3 E2
Tavistock 2 C3
Tayinloan 12 A3
Taynuilt 12 B1
Teignmouth 3 D3
Telford 7 E2
Tenbury Wells 7 E3
Tenby 2 B1
Tenterden 5 E3
Tetbury 3 F1
Tewkesbury 7 E4
Thame 4 B2
The Mumbles 2 C1
Thetford 9 E3
Thirsk 11 D2
Thornaby-on-Tees 11 D2
Thornbury 3 E1
Thorne 11 E4
Thorney 8 C3
Thornhill 13 D3
Thornton 10 B3
Thrapston 8 C3
Thurmaston 8 B3
Thursby 10 B1
Thurso 15 E1
Tickhill 11 D4
Tigh A Ghearraidh 14 A2
Tighnabruaich 12 B2
Tilbury 5 D2
Tillicoultry 13 D2
Tintagel 2 B3
Tiptree 5 E1
Tiverton 3 D2
Tobermory 12 A1
Todmorden 10 C4
Toft 13 F1
Tomatin 15 D3
Tomintoul 15 E3
Tonbridge 5 D3
Tongue 15 D1
Topsham 3 D3
Torpoint 2 C4
Torquay 3 D3
Totnes 3 D3
Totton 4 B4
Tow Law 10 C1
Towcester 4 B1

Tranent 13 D2
Trecastle 6 C4
Tredegar 7 D4
Tregaron 6 C3
Tring 4 C2
Troon 12 C3
Trowbridge 3 F1
Truro 2 B4
Tunstall 7 E1
Turriff 15 F3
Two Bridges 2 C3
Tynemouth 11 D1
Tywyn 6 C2

U
Uckfield 5 D3
Uffculme 3 D2
Uig 14 B2
Ullapool 14 C2
Ulsta 13 F1
Ulverston 10 B3
Upavon 4 A3
Upper Largo 13 D2
Uppingham 8 C3
Upton-upon-Severn 7 E4
Usk 7 D4
Uttoxeter 7 F2

V
Ventnor 4 B4
Voe 13 F1

W
Wadebridge 2 B3
Wainfleet All Saints 9 D2
Wakefield 11 D4
Wallasey 10 B4
Wallingford 4 B2
Walmer 5 F3
Walsall 7 F2
Waltham Abbey 5 D2
Walton on the Naze 5 F1
Wansford 8 C3
Wantage 4 B2
Ware 5 D1
Wareham 3 F3
Warminster 3 F2
Warrington 10 B4
Warwick 7 F3
Washington 11 D1
Watchet 3 D2
Watford 4 C2
Watton 9 E3
Weedon Bec 4 B1
Wellingborough 8 C4
Wellington *(Som)* 3 D2
Wellington *(Wrek)* 7 E2
Wells 3 E2
Wells-next-the-Sea 9 E2
Welshpool (Y Trallwng)
 7 D2
Welwyn Garden City 4 C2
Wem 7 E2
Wemyss Bay 12 B2
Wendover 4 C2
West Bridgford 8 B2
West Bromwich 7 F3
West Kilbride 12 B2
West Mersea 5 E2
Westbury 3 F2
Weston-super-Mare 3 E1
Westward Ho! 2 C2
Wetherby 11 D3
Weybridge 4 C3
Weymouth 3 F3
Whaley Bridge 7 F1
Wheatley 4 B2
Whipsnade 4 C1

Whitburn 13 D2
Whitby 11 E2
Whitchurch *(Bucks)* 4 B1
Whitchurch *(Hants)* 4 B3
Whitchurch *(Shrop)* 7 E2
Whitehaven 10 A2
Whithorn 12 C4
Whitley Bay 11 D1
Whitstable 5 E2
Whittington 7 D2
Whittlesey 8 C3
Wick 15 E1
Wickford 5 E2
Wickham Market 5 F1
Widecombe 2 C3
Widnes 7 E1
Wigan 10 B4
Wigston 8 B3
Wigton 10 A1
Wigtown 12 C4
Williton 3 D2
Wilmslow 7 E1
Wilton 4 A3
Wimborne Minster 4 A4
Wincanton 3 F2
Winchcombe 4 A1
Winchester 4 B3
Windermere 10 B2
Windsor 4 C2
Winsford 7 E1
Winslow 4 B1
Winterton 11 E4
Winterton-on-Sea 9 F2
Wirksworth 7 F1
Wisbech 9 D3
Wishaw 12 C2
Witham 5 E1
Withernsea 11 F4
Witney 4 B2
Wiveliscombe 3 D2
Wivenhoe 5 E1
Woburn 4 C1
Woking 4 C3
Wokingham 4 C2
Wolverhampton 7 E2
Wolverton 4 B1
Woodbridge 5 F1
Woodhall Spa 8 C2
Woodstock 4 B2
Woofferton 7 E3
Woolacombe 2 C2
Wooler 13 E3
Woore 7 E2
Wootton Bassett 4 A2
Worcester 7 E3
Workington 10 A1
Worksop 8 B1
Worthing 4 C4
Wotton-under-Edge 3 F1
Wragby 8 C1
Wrexham 7 D1
Wrotham 5 D3
Wroughton 4 A2
Wroxham 9 F3
Wymondham 9 E3

Y
Yarmouth 4 B4
Yate 3 F1
Yeadon 10 C3
Yeovil 3 E2
York 11 D3
Ystrad 3 D1

The Terms and Conditions detailed below apply to all Short Breaks and Holidays featured in this guide. Heritage is a division of Forte Hotels. When you make a booking, your contract will be with Forte (UK) Ltd ('Forte'), 166 High Holborn, London, WC1V 6TT.

1. Availability

All Short Breaks and Holidays featured in this guide are offered subject to availability. Bookings may be made for stays commencing from April 1st 2000 to March 31 2001 inclusive, excluding December 24th to 26th and December 31st to January 2nd. For a copy of our Christmas and New Year Celebrations brochure, please call 0345 700 350 quoting MH1.

Guide details apply to reservations made on or before March 31 2001 subject to publication of subsequent editions.

2. Holiday Types & Length of Stay

The main holiday types are:
Weekend Leisure Break – one or more consecutive nights between Friday and Sunday inclusive. (Weekend Leisure Breaks also include Bank Holiday Mondays.)

Midweek Leisure Break – one or more consecutive nights between Monday and Thursday.

Half Price Sunday Nights – If you book a Weekend Leisure Break on either a bed and breakfast or bed and breakfast basis for a Friday and Saturday night, you may stay on Sunday night at 50% of the Weekend Leisure Break price.

Weekaways – a great value bed and breakfast package for 5 nights or more – a 20% reduction on normal bed and breakfast prices

One night stays are available on all products featured in this guide except Half Price Sunday Nights and Weekaways.

3. Pricing & What's Included

All prices shown in this guide are in £'s per person per night (unless otherwise indicated) sharing a twin/double room or for one person in a single room. If staying as a single guest, a single occupancy supplement may apply (please see Single Guests below). For further information, please see the hotel listing information pricing panels, or call Forte Central Reservations on 0345 40 40 40.

All Short Breaks and Holidays prices in this guide include all taxes and non-optional service charges. Forte reserves the right to increase or decrease brochure prices to reflect any change in tax rates which occur after May 1st 2000. Once your contract is concluded, there will be no price changes.

Touring Holidays

'Touring Holidays' are for a minimum of 5 consecutive nights, and itineraries are tailor made to your individual requirements. Once you have planned your route and chosen your hotels from this guide, please call Heritage Inclusive Packages on 0345 543 555 who will calculate the price of your holiday.

Heritage Hotels 'Break for Murder'

All 'Break for Murder' weekends include a welcome reception, two nights' accommodation sharing a twin or double room with private en-suite bathroom (or a single room for single guests) colour television, telephone, tea and coffee making facilities, full traditional breakfast each morning, three course evening meal with coffee, and lunch on Saturday. Weekends also include a 'Break for Murder' programme with competitions, games and 'murders' appropriate to each plot, with actors to provide the entertainment and guide you through the murder plot.

'Break for Murder' operates according to a minimum and maximum group size to ensure that all participants benefit fully from the programme. If the appropriate numbers are not achieved, Forte reserve the right to cancel the break by giving at least two weeks' advance notice (usually longer) and, where possible, offering an alternative date or venue. Should these alternatives not be suitable, all moneys paid will be refunded. 'Break for Murder' is not suitable for children under 16.

Heritage Hotels 'Music at Leisure'

'Music at Leisure' weekends include two recitals and full programmes, a champagne reception on Friday and Saturday evenings, two nights' accommodation sharing a twin or double room with private en-suite bathroom (or a single room for single guests), colour television, telephone, tea and coffee making facilities, full traditional breakfast each morning, and three course evening meal with coffee. The weekends operate according to minimum party size. If the appropriate numbers are not achieved, Forte reserve the right to cancel the break by giving at least two weeks' advance notice (usually longer) and, where possible, offering an alternative date or venue. Should these alternatives not be suitable, all moneys paid will be refunded.

4. Meal Arrangements

All Short Breaks and Holidays which include breakfast offer a full traditional or Continental breakfast with tea or coffee.

All Short Breaks and Holidays which include dinner offer a choice from the hotel's three course evening menu. If an hotel does not provide a three course menu, guests may select a recognised starter, main course and dessert. A la carte dining is available at some hotels for an extra charge. All dinners include tea or coffee. Additional beverages are chargeable extras.

There is no refund for meals not taken, and lunch cannot be taken in place of dinner.

5. Tea & Coffee Making Facilities

Tea and coffee making facilities are available at all Heritage hotels. At The Randolph Hotel in Oxford and The Bath Spa Hotel in Bath, tea and coffee making facilities should be requested on arrival.

6. Feature Rooms

At many Heritage hotels, you may upgrade your accommodation to a feature room from £7.50 per person per night. Feature rooms may have a spectacular view, extra facilities or a four poster or half tester bed.

7. Single Guests

Individual guests using a single room are charged the standard per person rate as shown in the price panel. When no single room is available, individual guests may book a double or twin room and a sole occupancy charge will apply. Please ask for advice at the time of booking.

8. Children

At all Heritage hotels, up to 2 children under 16 stay free when sharing a suitable room with 1 or 2 adults, subject to availability. Children who occupy their own room will be charged 75% of the appropriate adult inclusive price. Children's meals will be charged as taken. Children aged 5 or under eat free. Cots and high chairs are available free of charge at all hotels.

9. Baby Listening & Baby Sitting

Baby listening is available free of charge at most hotels where advance notice is given. At some hotels, baby sitting is also available as a chargeable extra. Where available, 14 days' advance notice is required by calling the hotel direct. For more information on any individual hotel, please call Heritage Central Reservations on 0870 400 8855.

10. Guests with Impaired Mobility

A number of Heritage hotels offer modified facilities for guests with impaired mobility. Others, whilst not having special facilities, have mainly level access to public areas and accessible bathrooms. Please call Heritage Central Reservations on 0870 400 8855 for further information on the facilities at the hotel where you intend to stay.

11. Dogs

Certain Heritage hotels can accommodate dogs, at the manager's discretion, in some cases for an extra charge. Please call Heritage Central Reservations on 0870 400 8855 to enquire about the hotel where you intend to stay. All Heritage hotels accept guide dogs at no extra charge. Dogs are not allowed in the public areas (except guide dogs) and owners are responsible for making good the cost of any damage.

12. Car Parking

Car parking is free at most Heritage hotels, but at some sites there is limited availability. For further information on parking availability and charges, please call direct to the hotel of your intended stay on its enquiries number.

13. Checking In & Checking Out

Arrival

Hotel rooms are available from 14:00 on the day of arrival. Guests are asked to inform the hotel if arrival after 18:00 is anticipated.

Departure

Rooms must be vacated by 12:00 on the day of departure unless otherwise sanctioned at the discretion of the Hotel Manager.

14. Health and Fitness Clubs

A charge may be made for the use of certain facilities; e.g. solaria, exercise classes and beauty treatments, where available.

Under 16's are not permitted to use the gymnasium and must be accompanied by a responsible adult at all times when using the other facilities.

Under 5's are not permitted to use spa pools, saunas, solaria or steam rooms.

15. General Information

All information is correct as at March 1st 2000 but is subject to change before your contract is concluded.

The photographs, illustrations and descriptions of facilities, amenities, surrounding areas and places of interest are reproduced in this guide to give a general impression of what to expect on your chosen short break or holiday and should not be taken as a guarantee of what will be available.

Heritage cannot be held responsible for events beyond its control or the control of its suppliers (such as fire, strikes, industrial action, terrorist activity, technical problems with transport, illness of entertainers and/or sporting supervisors and bad weather), nor for any curtailment, cancellation or change to any accommodation, activity or itinerary which is caused as a result of such events.

16. Complaints & Comments

Any complaint or comment regarding a stay at an hotel should be made to that hotel's Duty Manager at the time of the visit so that it can be resolved on the spot. Problems which cannot be resolved there and then should be notified in writing, within 28 days of departure, to the following: Managing Director, Heritage Hotels, 166 High Holborn, London WC1V 6TT.

BOOKING INFORMATION

1. How to Book

There are four ways to make a booking:-
Call Heritage Central Reservations on 0870 400 8855; or
Call the hotel of your intended stay; or
Contact your travel agent; or
For Touring Holidays, Murder Breaks and Music at Leisure packages, call Heritage Inclusive Packages on 0345 543555

If you make a booking through Heritage Central Reservations or direct with the hotel, you will be asked to guarantee your booking with a credit/debit card. If you do not possess a credit/debit card, you will be required to pre-pay by cheque (made payable to Forte (UK) Ltd). To pre-pay by cheque, please contact Heritage Central Reservations for a booking form, complete and sign this form and send it along with your cheque to the hotel of your intended stay. Alternatively, send your cheque with a covering letter stating your arrival and departure dates to the hotel of your intended stay. You will find the address printed in the hotel listing information. Where pre-payment by cheque is necessary, at least three working days following receipt of

your cheque will be required to process the transaction prior to your stay commencing.

If you make a Touring Holiday booking through Forte Inclusive Packages on 0345 543 555, you will be required to pre-pay in full for your break. For Murder Breaks and Music at Leisure weekends, a deposit of 20% is required. Please contact Heritage Central Reservations for a booking form, complete and sign this form, and send it along with your credit/debit card details, or a cheque made payable to Forte (UK) Ltd, to Forte Inclusive Packages, Oak Court, Dudley Road, Brierly Hill, West Midlands DY5 1LG. Where pre-payment is by cheque, at least three working days will be required following receipt of your cheque to process the transaction prior to your stay commencing.

If you make a booking through a travel agent, please contact Heritage Central Reservations for a booking form, complete and sign this form, including your payment details, and give this to your travel agent. Your travel agent will do the rest.

2. Important Information Regarding Availability

Heavy demand at certain times of the year may mean that some rooms may not be available at the special prices featured in this guide. In the case of facilities/services not provided by Forte, prices are subject to change before the contract is concluded. Forte will inform guests of these changes. Your travel agent will be pleased to confirm and offer alternative dates and hotels if necessary. Receipt of payment does not guarantee availability.

3. Deposits & Pre-Payment

Bookings made through Forte Central Reservations or with the hotel direct

Deposits and pre-payments are not required for most of the Short Breaks and Holidays featured in this guide. Deposits and pre-payments are, however, required when making bookings for all Touring Holidays, Murder Breaks and Music at Leisure weekends.

When booking a Touring Holiday, the full price of the holiday and the special delivery post supplement must be pre-paid in full prior to your stay commencing. Payment can be made by credit/debit card or by cheque (made payable to Forte (UK) Ltd) to Forte Inclusive Packages, Oak Court, Dudley Road, Brierley Hill, West Midlands DY5 1LG.

When booking a Heritage Hotels 'Break for Murder' or 'Music at Leisure' weekend, a deposit of 20% of the holiday price is required. Payment by credit/debit card or cheque (made payable to Forte (UK) Ltd) should be sent to the hotel direct, and the address will be advised at the time of making the booking.

4. Balance of Moneys Outstanding

Prior to your departure from the hotel you will be required to settle your bill. If your reservation was made through a travel agent, you will be required to pay for all extra services consumed during your stay that were not included in your pre-paid Short Break or Holiday. If your reservation was made direct with Forte, you will be required to pay for the

Short Break or Holiday in full, less any pre-payments, plus any extra services consumed during your stay.

On arrival, you will be asked to produce a valid credit card for the hotel to take an imprint. Forte accepts all major credit cards, including MasterCard, Visa, American Express and Diners Club. Alternatively, payment may be made by cheque, payable to Forte (UK) Ltd. All cheques must be supported by, and within the limits of, a current cheque card; above this limit they are accepted only by prior arrangement with the hotel. Where pre-payment by cheque is necessary, at least three working days will be required to process the transaction.

5. Cancellations & Amendments
Tickets

Once issued, all tickets for theatre performances, concerts and events booked through Heritage cannot be amended and no refunds will paid.

There is no charge if you wish to cancel any other booking up to 14:00 on the day of arrival. In the event of cancellation after 14:00 or non-arrival, Heritage reserves the right to charge you for one night's accommodation.

In the event of a guest cancelling 'Touring Holidays', 'Music at Leisure' and 'Break for Murder' holidays, 20% of the total holiday price will be retained as a cancellation charge. A cancellation reference will be given and should be retained.

Refund of Moneys Paid

The balance of moneys paid, less any cancellation charges and the cost of any tickets, will be refunded on receipt of all documentation and tickets either by your travel agent or at Forte (UK) Ltd, Oak Court, Dudley Road, Brierley Hill, West Midlands DY5 1LG.

6. Holiday & Travel Insurance

Forte (UK) Ltd strongly recommend that all guests take out adequate holiday/travel insurance when booking any of the short breaks and holidays featured in this guide. Forte (UK) Ltd have arranged a special facility with Aon Cork Bays & Fisher of Lloyds Chambers, 1 Portsoken Street, London E1 8DF. Please call 020 680 4000 or ask your travel agent for further information and prices.

7. Booking Afterthoughts

Should you have any post-booking queries, please call Heritage Central Reservations on 0870 400 8855, or the hotel direct, quoting your booking reference number. If your booking was made through a travel agent, please contact your travel agent and quote your booking reference number.

8. Security for Moneys Paid Over

Under Government regulations, Forte (UK) Ltd is required to provide insurance, in relation to certain packages, for security of money paid over by guests and for their repatriation in the unlikely event of insolvency of the company. This insurance is arranged by Aon Risk Services Ltd of Lloyds Chambers, 1 Portsoken Street, London E1 8DF Telephone 0207 680 4000.

Pictures reproduced with the kind permission of: